Shine the Light:
"Lessons in Daniel"

© By Dr. Randall D. Smith

"Scripture quotations taken from the New American Standard Bible®,
Copyright © 1960, 1962, 1963, 1968, 1971, 1972, 1973,
1975, 1977, 1995 by The Lockman Foundation
Used by permission." (www.Lockman.org)

These volumes were prepared with students and teachers of the Bible in mind. The series is taken from the actual teaching notes of Dr. Smith as he teaches through all of the Bible each year at Great Commission Bible Institute in Sebring, Florida.

Shine the Light:
Lessons in Daniel

Lesson One: Daniel 1:1-21 "Finding the Missing Smile"

> Key Principle: Because life is filled with negative people and situations does not mean the believer should be negative

Lessons Two: Daniel 2:1-23 "Six Positive Truths about Life's Problems"

> Key Principle: Adversity can be another tool for shaping our lives in the hands of a creative God!

Lesson Three: Daniel 3:1-30 "The Puppet Masters"

> Key Principle: Dark times are unique opportunities for piercing light to make a real difference!

Lesson Four: Daniel 4:1-27 "Seven Steps to Effective Sharing of Truth"

> Key Principle: Effective outreach is when the world about us can truly hear what we are trying to say and respond correctly to it.

Lesson Five: Daniel 5:1-31 "Rescue from the Forgotten"

> Key Principle: To offer a positive message, we must stay engaged in the world that needs truth while longing for the life to come

Lesson Six: Daniel 6:1-28 "Five Critical Choices"

Key Principle: Your ability to be positive has more to do with your life choices than your life circumstances!

Lesson Seven: Daniel 2:19-45 "Revealing the Weakness"

Key Principle: God is working a plan through kings and kingdoms (governments) – but human government won't ultimately fix what is broken – because it can't.

Lesson Eight: Daniel 7:1-28 "Facing a Nightmare"

Key Principle: The struggle for a righteous kingdom will continue until God establishes His kingdom on Earth in place of the works of men.

Lesson Nine: Daniel 8:1-27 "Seeing with New Eyes"

Key Principle: The mature believer's view of the world should not be about the grasp of darkness, but rather about God at work moving history toward His purposes.

Lesson Ten: Daniel 9:1-24 "Off the Bench" (Part One)
Key Principle: At the heart of our walk with God there are DISCIPLINES of our walk and PROMISES of our God.

Lesson Eleven: Daniel 9-12 "Peering into the Darkness"

Key Principle: History is "His" story – and God is never surprised by it.

Lesson Twelve: Daniel 10:1-21 "Sock Puppets"

Key Principle: We gain courage and proper perspective when we recognize the physical world is not the only world, and not the real world. What we see, feel, and experience, is often caused by something we cannot see from a spiritual world well hidden.

*Note the book order was altered at the end to follow Daniel's life, and end in chapter 10, with the last recorded events of his life.

Table of Contents

Background Notes: 9

Lesson One: Daniel 1:1-21 "Finding the Missing Smile" 17

Lesson Two: Daniel 2:1-23 "Six Positive Truths about Life's Problems" 33

Lesson Three: Daniel 3:1-30 "The Puppet Masters" 49

Lesson Four: Daniel 4:1-27 "Seven Steps to Effective Sharing of Truth" 63

Lesson Five: Daniel 5:1-31 "Rescue from the Forgotten" 79

Lesson Six: Daniel 6:1-28 "Five Critical Choices" 95

Lesson Seven: Daniel 2:19-45 "Revealing the Weakness" 109

Lesson Eight: Daniel 7:1-28 "Facing a Nightmare" 123

Lesson Nine: Daniel 8:1-27 "Seeing with New Eyes" 139

Lesson Ten: Daniel 9:1-24 "Off the Bench" (Part One) 155

Lesson Eleven: Daniel 9-12 "Peering into the Darkness" 173

Lesson Twelve: Daniel 10:1- 21 "Sock Puppets" 189

8

Shine the Light
Lessons in Daniel

Background Notes:
A Few Words to Introduce the Book of Daniel

Let's begin with a general note about the book that may make its twelve chapters more comprehensible. Daniel is unique in the Bible as it was passed down to us in two different languages, and may have been originally authored that way. In addition, it was also written in a narrative that is easily divisible into two sections:

- Section One: A review of Chapters 1-7 are GENTILE LESSONS ON DANIEL'S FAITH (Daniel 2:4-7:28 was presumably written in the Aramaic language).

- Section Two: A review of Chapters 8-12 are ISRAEL'S LESSONS FROM DANIEL'S EXPERIENCE (Daniel 8-12 was presumably written in the Hebrew language).

We assume the sections written in Aramaic were for a more "public" Gentile mass consumption, and the parts in Hebrew were more specific to the future of the Jewish people and prophetic materials related primarily to them. If that is true, part of the book is like an evangelistic "tract" for the God of Abraham to a pagan culture – making the first part of the book lessons in "becoming a light" to lost people. The second part of the book records specific prophetic materials essential to encourage and educate the Jewish people.

Daniel - The Man:

It is also worth a few moments to consider some thoughts about the prophet Daniel based on the Biblical materials we have. First, his name means "God is my Judge". He is (at present in arcaeology) unknown outside of the text that bears his name (in contemporary historical writings or primary source materials).

We have no coins with his picture or epigraphic inscriptions with his name in the dedication. Therefore, our whole picture of Daniel must be derived from the Bible. Here is what we have:

He was from an aristocratic family (Daniel 1:3), and was carried into Babylon by Nebuchadnezzar II (Daniel 1:1) in the third year (4th by Jewish reckoning) of Jehoiakim's reign. Born in "Eretz Israel" (the land of Israel) most likely in Judah, he entered the world during the reforms of king Josiah c. 621BCE and lived at least until about 536 BCE. He was part of the first Jewish exiles to be taken captive into Babylon from Judah (606 BCE).

God honored Daniel and gave him great understanding to qualify as one of the "wise men" (Daniel 1:20; 2:13) of the nation. He was given the gift of dreams, visions and their interpretation. In the narrative, his Babylonian name was Belteshazzar (Daniel 1:7) meaning 'may Bel protect his life'. Ironically, God later saved his life and the life of all the other wise men of Babylon condemned to death (Daniel 2:1-13) when he was enabled by God to tell the king Nebuchadnezzar his dream and its interpretation (Daniel 2:14-30).

Daniel was used of God to foretell the end of the Babylonian kingdom, and the dividing of the kingdom between the Medes and the Persians. After the transfer of power to the Persians, Daniel served as one of the three "presidents" of Medo-Persia administrating over princes who ruled over 129 provinces. He was (at that time) over eighty years old and was being considered by Darius for promotion over the other two presidents (Daniel 6:1-3). Thus throughout his lifetime, Daniel offered a great example of a man who fearlessly worshipped the God of Israel even in exile away from the Temple worship and sacrifice.

His name appears apart from the book of Daniel in the book of Ezekiel (Ezekiel 14:14) with reference to his righteousness and in the Gospel accounts of Matthew and Mark with reference to the end time prophecy. He received many visions and was ministered to by heaven's archangels, Gabriel and Michael (Daniel 8:16-17; 9:21; 10:13; 12:1). He may well have had visits of the Pre-incarnate Christ Who appeared to him by the Tigris river and in the lion's den (scholars debate if this was Christ, but the appearances were recorded in Daniel 6:22; 10:4-9,16,17).

The Times:

Some records of two great empires of Mesopotamia are found within his writings.

First, there are records of the Kingdom of Babylon:

- Nabopolassar (625-605) during first wave of captivity (before Daniel is taken).

- *Nebuchadnezzar II (605-562)* son of predecessor; *took Daniel captive in successsive waves.*

- Amil (Evil) Merodach (562-560; cp. 2 Ki. 25:27f) reigns only 2 Years, slain by brother-in-law.

- Nergelsharuzar (560-556) [cPo Jer. 39:3J; - seized throne from brother-in-law; a builder and administrator; left throne to son.

- Lubashi-Merodach (556 BCE) child king murdered within nine months.

- Nabonidus (556-539) a general and skilled tactician; but poor politician. He rebuilt temples of older gods. This offended contemporary priests and lost popular support that paved the way for the Medo-Persian conquest to be invited by the masses.

    (Regent) Belshazzar, *son* of Nabonidus and holder of the crown for his father during his many military exploits (ruled 549 until 539 takeover by Persian Cyrus II); and administrator of the empire while his father stayed at Teima in western Arabia in the latter years.

Second, there are records concerning the Kingdom of the Medians and the Persians:

The earliest record of the Persians that scholars have widely accepted was an Assyrian inscription that may be from about 850 BCE. The inscription is important because it notes both this group, called the Parsu, and the nearby Madai (Medians). Both tribes were brought under the control of the Assyrians (Sargon annexed the Parsuash- region of the Parsu- in 719 BCE. The Madai rose to self control, then eventual domination of the Parsu in what is now called the Median Empire (728-550 BCE).

- Cyrus II (560-530 BCE) *son* of Cambyses I the Persian. His father had been dominated by Astyages the Mede, and married Astyages' daughter. Cyrus II was their offspring. Cyrus rebelled against Asytages' dominion, and took Ekbatana (Astyages capital). He established Persian supremacy, but allowed Astyages to live making him uncharacteristically humane. Cyrus became the Shah (King) of a unified Persian kingdom. Cyrus then led the united Medes and Persians to the conquest of the Lydian Kingdom, and eventually (by 539 BCE) to Babylon. Following the victory, Cyrus set organized the Empire under a new charter of human rights called the Cyrus Cylinder. Perhaps this tendency for a "soft spot" demonstrates his willingness expressed in allowing the **Jews to begin to return to Israel**. Cyrus was killed in 530 BCE during a battle.

    **Darius the Mede (cp. Daniel 5:30) appeared during the reign of Cyrus; most scholars currently identify him as Gubaru, Darius being only a title for governor (though this is uncertain). He may be the ruling name for Cyrus in Babylon, or may be a governor placed by Cyrus.

Outside the Scope of Daniel: The Persian Empire had known rulers:

- Cambyses II (also called Bardiya) son of Cyrus the Great (Cyrus II); reigns about 8 years until about 522 BCE. He annexed Egypt into the empire, but was killed by Darius I.

- Darius I (the Great) 522-486, son of Hystaspes fought the rebel Gautama and prevailed, while gaining popular strength. After his rise to Shah, he led armies to the Indus River, Thrace, and even into Greece. With a sprawling empire, he divided the land into twenty satrapies, and personally appointed each ruler. He expanded the mail system of the Assyrians before him, and increased trade, securing routes throughout the empire. He was eventually defeated at Marathon by the Greeks (491) and returned to empire humiliated. It may be during this time the Zoroastrian tradition gained great ground in the empire. Clearly, this religio-philosophical system eventually dominated the region (Note: the rise of "free will").

- Xerxes I (cp. Esther) the son of Darius I; had the great aim to defeat the Greeks but lost at
- The Battle of Platea in 479 BCE. He returned to build Persepolis in humiliation (in which the chapters 2ff of Esther occur).

- Artaxerxes I Longimanus (465-423). Darius II 423-404. Artaxerxes II Minemnon (404-359) (cp. Nehemiah).

- Artaxerxes III Ochus (359-338); Arses, (338-335) ; Darius III, (335-331?) defeated by Alexander the Great. Greek Domination begins...

The Writing: The Purpose of the Book of Daniel

One can never assume to know exactly why any author writes what he does, especially when the author is superintended by the Spirit of the Most High God. There are, however, clues that will build evidence toward a number of conclusions that can focus the purpose of the book more clearly for the student. Some clues worth considering are:

As we suggested in the very beginning of our study, Daniel appears to have been a **bilingual** writing, with a Hebrew introduction and ending (1:1-2:4a; 8-12 respectively). The other portion of the book is in Aramaic, the common diplomatic Gentile language of his day (2:4b-7:28). In addition, Daniel appears to be **thematically** demonstrating the superiority of "El Elyon" (the Most High God) over Gentiles as well as His own people – the Hebrews – especially seen as the Aramaic section of the book unfolds. The book's theme appear to **shift** in emphasis when the Hebrew language resumes in chapter 8, to a program of God's dealing with his people not only in chastisement, but in future restoration and prominence.

As a result, we can reasonably conclude that Daniel appears to be written to convey a very practical message to a lost world of heathen men - **El Elyon rules in the kingdom of men**, even in a kingdom that refuses to acknowledge consistently His strength. Additionally, the message of the book to the Hebrew was predictive and prophetic, and includes the time of God's blessed restoration of His people to their home and worship center. There are, of course, prophecies in the "practical" section (the Aramaic portion), as well as "prophetic" parts in the "practical" section (cp. chapter 2 and 7). Notwithstanding, these general sections may help to guide us in the overall tone and theme(s) of this writing.

Let's suggest, then, a summary statement of the work's purpose:

To encourage exilic Jews and subsequent generations by outlining future destructions of Gentile world powers and the rise of the Messianic Kingdom.

The Writing: Critical Notes on Authorship

The book has been criticized over the centuries and its authenticity has been tested. Let's take a moment to acknowledge the debate and offer a few introductory comments about its veracity.

First, there were questions about the Authorship of Daniel as authentic to "Daniel the Statesman" (a literal view of the author as stated in the text). The reasons cited for accepting the literal position are: The book was attested in Jewish and Christian tradition. In this view, Jews would have known if his authorship was forged, the hope the book offered was false. In addition, the work appears to be attested in Dead Sea scrolls, 150 BCE, as we have a fragment containing Daniel in the collection. Since it would have taken time before the writings were counted as scripture and recorded, this lends itself to an early acceptance and early date – though not numbers can be affixed to the date of the original through the extant copy.

There have been <u>Historical critical reviews</u> that generally follow five common objections to the author and writing:

Historical critics cite the work labeled **Daniel was not included in the section called the "Prophets"** (Nevi'im) but in "Writings" (Kotavim) in the Hebrew canon. Yet three answers have been offered as rebuttal:

- There is no evidence one section closed after another.
- The Book of Samuel is a historical book in the "Prophets" section.
- Daniel was not a prophet but a statesman with the gift of prophecy – which may explain the placement.

In addition, **Apocryphal lists** failed to include Daniel as an O.T. character. Yet, conservative scholars argue rightly that there are others who are not mentioned either.

A third objection is that some scholars indicated that Daniel contained (in their view) **supposed errors about the 6th century** B.C.E. Yet a careful examination of each offers hope to the literalist:

- Chapter 1:1 mentioned a deportation under **Jehoiakim**. The Book of 2 Kings didn't note. Note: Other sources confirm this event. (George Smith in his works on Assyria).

- Daniel 1:1 recorded Nebuchadnezzar is in the **3rd** year of the reign of Jehoiakim. Jeremiah says the 4th. Note: There were two ways of calculation of calendar.

- Daniel recorded Belshazzar as the **son** of Nebuchadnezzar, but that detail is untrue - there were generations in between. Yet, to the Bible student, we know that the term "son" was often used to denote "successor of" and not only immediate offspring.

- Daniel recorded **Belshazzar was king**, but actually Nabonidus was king. It is worth noting that some Babylonian records say Nebuchadnezzar made his son, Belshazzar co-regent. There is much we do not have in detail about the times.

- Archaeology offers no detail on **Darius the Mede** from that time. Yet, scholars are willing to wait and see what the future holds. In the past, archaeology offered no details on Pontius Pilate (until 1960), the Sargon and or the people called "Hittites" (until Hattusa was discovered).

- Critics have questioned the use of **Greek words** in Daniel's account. The three Greek words in Daniel 3:5 are all musical terms. It is worth noting that Nebuchadnezzar had Greek soldiers and the words were out of use by the time of the LXX – offering evidence for an early date of the original!

- The **Jewish theology** of Messiah, angels and resurrection are often thought to have been much more elemental and underdeveloped by 600 BCE, and that has raised critical hackles in some. Yet, scholars at the same time admit that "Jewish theology" is a misnomer. Such ideas were mentioned in Isaiah – but critical scholarship simply dates these to late additions as well.

In summation, historical critics of Daniel refuse to believe because the book predictively describes the Greek period (Hasmonean and Maccabee periods) in Israel in detail. At the same time, scholars must admit that the Dan. 9: 20-27 vision includes details up to the time that Messiah is cut off and Jerusalem is destroyed, which are valid prophecy, but the text existed in the Dead Sea Scrolls collection from more than two hundred years prior to the fall of Jerusalem under Rome – a confirmation of predictive prophecy.

Let's move now into the book of Daniel to learn how to SHINE THE LIGHT in a dark world!

Shine the Light
Lessons in Daniel

Lesson One: Daniel 1:1-21 "Finding the Missing Smile"

How is your smile these days? The market is flooded with dentifrices that can improve the condition of your teeth, but that isn't the same thing as improving your smile. You see, a smile is more than showing your teeth – that can be a symbol of hostility and not friendship! A smile is more than the uptick at the corners of your lips – some very grumpy people have that as a natural feature. **Your smile comes from within if it is real.**

How are you doing on the ENCOURAGEMENT side of life? Do you feel beat down by the news surrounding you? Are your friends sharing more and more about illnesses and troubles with you? Are you finding it harder to find peace and happiness in a world charged by extreme voices? Is everything in your life becoming more painfully divided – red state, blue state, conservative, liberal, "pro" this and "anti" that? Are you having a harder time keeping a positive attitude when negativity seems so willing to swirl and curl around your feet like a slithering python?

Maybe the problem isn't where you live, but where you choose to draw encouragement – and that is what we want to explore today in the first chapter of Daniel. Let me set up the story…

Four young men found themselves far from home and surrounded on a campus by pagan parties and godless professors – but they made a difference with their lives that affected their whole nation. How did this happen? **They made a singular choice: they would not be pressed into the mold of their times. They took God's Word seriously, and lived it in front of people who knew little of their God, and had no**

respect for their beliefs. The four young men did not become belligerent, but did not blend in either. <u>They walked with God when few others did – and that choice made all the difference.</u>

The answer to lasting encouragement is not acquiescing to the world. The answer is not blending into popular opinion. Most believers have enough grounding in the Spirit to know that. At the same time, the answer is NOT found in stubbornness and irritability either.

The answer is found in coming to peace through the discovery of "wisdom from above." Looking at life through the window of God's wisdom will restore a lasting smile to our face. It is time to smile again!

Look for a moment at *James 3:13-18*:

3:13 Who among you is wise and understanding? Let him show by his good behavior his deeds in the gentleness of wisdom. 14 But if you have bitter jealousy and selfish ambition in your heart, do not be arrogant and so lie against the truth. 15 This wisdom is not that which comes down from above, but is earthly, natural, demonic. 16 For where jealousy and selfish ambition exist, there is disorder and every evil thing. 17 But the wisdom from above is first pure, then peaceable, gentle, reasonable, full of mercy and good fruits, unwavering, without hypocrisy. 18 And the seed whose fruit is righteousness is sown in peace by those who make peace.

James said, in effect, "Walk softly and with a calm compassion among lost men." Consider their plight – to view only the shadows of truth through darkened windows; to hear only muffled sounds of broken conversation from a great distance.

Remember, our life has been forever changed by encountering our Creator. We stand in the gentle rain of God's wisdom – unique, clean, crisp and clear. We experience the cleansing touch of the Creator – being washed by love and warmly embraced as a loved child. Our work now is to learn gentleness that we may sow calmly and yield fruit approved by the One Who called us to this work. Only those who show peace will truly be able to offer peace.

Let me say it another way…

Key Principle: Because life is filled with negative people and situations does not mean the believer should be negative.

Even in the garden with weeds, I farm in my gracious Father's field! **Our attitude truly effects our presentation of Jesus to the lost world…**so today we want to address that attitude, and how we can look at life differently.

Let's first recognize a few important concepts:

- **Our attitude is the tint you apply to the windshield of your life.** You see through it according to that tint – and respond to what you see. The issue is that we put the tint on the glass. **Consciously or unconsciously – the tint is our doing.**

- **If you think carefully about it, there is very little that distinguishes one person from another that is not easily changed – hair color, shape, dress.** The one thing that can make the person stand out is their attitude! I suspect that many of us have encountered people who are lovely in physical form, but ugly in attitude. Their attempts to look nice were a waste – because their **attitude showed their lack of character – and that overshadowed all of their other beauty enhancements.**

- **Our attitude may be the single factor that has the biggest impact on people.** When we are hit with hardship, but answer with kindness – character is displayed through the instrument of good attitude.

- **It is our attitude that is perhaps the most important governing factor to how we handle adversity!**

Daniel, Hananiah, Mishael and Azaryahu were four young men who found themselves in the wrong place at the wrong time – from man's perspective.

- They were young – but surrounded by godless influences.
- They were smart – but they were placed into training in an academy founded on paganism and anti –Yahweh thinking.
- They were bound under the yoke of the world - yet they were used of God and powerful instruments in His hand.

How did they accomplish this? **They played life by a <u>set of rules</u> that we want to recognize today, because God preserved them for us:**

Rule 1: Recognize God's hand in your circumstances. (1:1-2)

You and I are in God's hand! See it in the perspective of God's control. Note: *"The Lord gave" (1:1-2).* Daniel's story began with a record that *"In the year 605 the capital city of my people was besieged" (1:1)* and *"we lost the battle." (1:2a) "Our king was taken into captivity and the temple sacked." (1:2)* Look at it closely:

Daniel 1:1 In the third year of the reign of Jehoiakim king of Judah, Nebuchadnezzar king of Babylon came to Jerusalem and besieged it. 2 The Lord gave Jehoiakim king of Judah into his hand, along with some of the vessels of the house of God; and he brought them to the land of Shinar, to the house of his god, and he brought the vessels into the treasury of his god.

We must recognize two very important truths:

First, life is out of my control.

A man who battled cancer for two years made this clear to me, "Doc, all the things that matter most in my life are the things I don't control at all." He continued: "Life's experiences were largely meant to bring us to the humbling point, where we could strip away our self-reliance and see our need for Christ."

He was right – we don't control the important things. The Christmas wedding that ended in a car accident that killed the bride this past week is a profound statement that our plans don't run the table in life.

Second, life is never out of God's control.

If my city is overrun by pagans, and my worship center sacked and closed to me – that doesn't mean that God lost control.

It means that God is choosing to speak through me, and not my culture. His requirement in my life is NOT LESSENED because there are fewer people around me that believe truth. He knows the time I was placed into – because His plan did the placing. When I bow my knee to His Sovereignty, I acknowledge before Him the right He possesses to direct the plan He has made.

The record of Daniel begins, not with a notice of DEFEAT, but a notice of **GOD AT WORK**.

That is the first step to dealing with my attitude. My countenance rises when I recognize that my circumstances have not victimized me – they are a part of the plan God made for me. That will straighten my posture and renew my confidence. I may not be in control, but God is never out of control!

When I was in High School, Sylvester Stallone was getting beat up in a boxing ring, and running up the steps of the Philadelphia Art Museum, lifting his hands high at the top of the steps – as Rocky Balboa. I don't recall most of the story. What I do recall is that at one point he was in the ring and being pummeled in the way that only Balboa could handle. Everyone thought he was losing – but his manager knew different. He said something like, "He isn't getting beaten; he's getting mad!" The point of that story is NOT that getting mad was a good thing – but rather the underlying truth. What looks like a defeat ISN'T if there is a plan underneath the gains and losses…

Let that sink in for a moment. When God is in the plan – there are no real "losses" or "victories" – ultimately there is only the plan. When we look at the situation in Central African Republic, we need to recognize that today. When we look at our courts peeling away from Scripture (and even common sense), we need to recall that. When we follow Him, we have the confidence He can use us in any way He chooses – and that is our delight, not simply our "veil of tears" burden!

Rule 2: Collect the knowledge you need to navigate well. (1:1-7)

Keep reading in Daniel 1:

Daniel 1:3 Then the king ordered Ashpenaz, the chief of his officials, to bring in some of the sons of Israel, including some of the royal family and of the nobles, 4 youths in whom was no defect, who were good-looking, showing intelligence in every [branch of] wisdom, endowed with understanding and discerning knowledge, and who had ability for serving in the king's court; and [he ordered him] to teach them the literature and language of the Chaldeans. 5 The king appointed for them a daily ration from the king's choice food and from the wine which he drank, and [appointed] that they should be educated three years, at the end of which they were to enter the king's personal service. 6 Now among them from the sons of Judah were Daniel, Hananiah, Mishael and Azariah. 7 Then the commander of the officials assigned [new] names to them; and to Daniel he assigned [the name] Belteshazzar, to

Hananiah Shadrach, to Mishael Meshach and to Azariah Abed-nego.

It is obvious that these four men would not be able to live out their lives in monastic isolation and the bubble of biblical training. Humanly speaking – they were captives. Their education was being deliberately staged and patterned by pagan thinkers – godless men in combination with idolaters – not a Yahwist in the lot! Home schooling wasn't "on the table." What to do?

That is where the second rule will come in handy. As believers, we will get along much better if we understand the situation surrounding us well, and comprehend the actual conditions we are living in – along with the requisite expectations (1:3-7). We must be BOTH students of the Word of God, and careful students of our times – viewing the world through the lens of opportunity to reach out in love and care.

How do we do that?

First, assume that EVERY PERSON can teach you something of value and you can learn important information in EVERY SITUATION!

If you start at the bottom of the work chain, you get the best view of every step of the work – if you will do what you do to the best of your abilities. If you and I truly value (and show it) even the person we disagree with the most, we will learn more and get into shouting matches less.

The internet is probably the WORST place for this, and the next-door neighbor the best. The internet is a great place for grouping – but not a sincere place for learning. Most of the so-called "information sources" aren't about balance and point-counterpoint argumentation – they are tailor-made for dedicated audiences of one side of a discussion. They quickly descend into SHOUT FESTS and NAME CALLING exhibitions – where we can see the most creative part of the discussion is the symbols people use to say vulgar words that would otherwise be excluded from the comment section. If only people would place as much emphasis on the thinking of their own argument.

Remember, everyone can teach you something – even if it is only a window into the thinking of a poorly formed argument. Don't insult people, even if they insult you. You can stop a discussion at any time, but don't make people feel small – it harms the Gospel.

Second, don't measure your effectiveness by societal symbols, but rather by personal interactions and obedient choices on behalf of Christ.

Here is where many a church went in the wrong direction during the years of my career. Some in the church thought our country was Christian, and therefore relaxed explaining the Gospel to their neighbors. They thought the job was being done on radio and TV, and if that wasn't enough – there were plenty of churches in town to do it. What they forgot was the Gospel isn't primarily accomplished by a media blitz – or Jesus would have just sent a video instead of coming. All the "Jesus Films" in the world won't transform the world. **Most of the time, the Gospel must be seen in a life before it is adopted in a new heart.** The films are a great help to teams that will present Christ in the flesh – but we cannot simply digitize the *Bible* and wait for people to adopt it – that WON'T work.

Others went the opposite direction. They measured Christianity's effectiveness by the size and budget of mega-churches. They counted the numbers of Promise Keeping men to measure our faith. Some of those same people assume, now that the "Crystal Cathedral" is defunct, that Christianity is 'on the ropes' – and they are wrong. It was ALREADY in deep trouble when the attendance, the corporation model, and its budget were the measure for the value of the truth the church contained.

A believer's identity isn't primarily found in outward symbols – church buildings, clerical costumes, attendance numbers at public rallies, etc. **Christianity is primarily seen in the daily lifestyle choices of those who know and follow Jesus Christ and His Word.** That is the argument of "sound doctrine" of Titus 2. Daniel and his friends knew the world could change their Hebrew names, but not take their Hebrew heart away from them.

Look at their names, just to recall their heritage:
Daniel 1:6 Among these were some from Judah...

> Daniel: name means "God is my judge"
> Hananiah: "The Lord has been gracious"
> Mishael: "The one who comes from God"
> Azariah: "The Lord is my helper"

Now look at what the chief official replaced the references to their God with as he gave them Babylonian names:

> Daniel, Belteshazzar: "The secret of their god Bel"
> Hananiah, Shadrach: "The inspiration of the sun god"
> Mishael, Meshach: "He who belongs to the goddess Sheshach"
> Azariah, Abednego: "Servant of Nebo – the morning star"

The world WILL NOT LONG TOLERATE any symbol that truly exalts God. Christmas will be reduced to "Winter Holiday" simply to extract the wonderful name that will one day make every knee bow. The fight to win a culture can only be won by a Christian community that will take on personal choices to live up to the standards of the Word. **Note that although the young people were given names of pagan gods of Babylon their lifestyle choices demonstrated their Hebrew names.**

Let me say it clearly to every believer: The Supreme Court doesn't truly harm Christianity as much as our public failure to live the standard of God's Word as believers. Their decisions may seem sweeping and vast, but they come on top of years of Christian lifestyle compromises that muted our voice and blunted our message.

Our churches speak of marriages, but many of our own don't stay committed to them. We speak of biblical education for our young, but cannot find enough people with time to be a part of a program where we could help teach them. The world won't be radically impacted by comfortable Christians – only committed ones who make comfort a secondary issue.

Make your testimony one that speaks to the true legacy of what is important to you. Expend yourself in things that God lays upon your heart!

Oscar Wilde was quoted years ago as saying: "If you don't get everything you want, think of the things you don't get that you don't want!" Look around you, and collect knowledge of the expectations, arguments and lifestyles – but keep living your call.

Rule 3: Keep your true life-goal at the center of your decision-making. (1:8)

Make up your mind that you will stand for God with a positive voice as He enables you and then attempt to work in the system to accomplish the task.

Daniel 1:8 But Daniel made up his mind that he would not defile himself with the king's choice food or with the wine which he drank; so he sought [permission] from the commander of the officials that he might not defile himself.

Here is the tough part of the line. Daniel couldn't do all that was being asked of him – so he needed to find a creative and sensitive way to object, without being belligerent.

The missionary Hudson Taylor demonstrated faith and inner calm in a challenging situation in 1853, when young Hudson Taylor was making his first voyage to China. His ship was delayed near New Guinea because the winds had stopped. A rapid current was carrying the ship toward some reefs and the situation was becoming dangerous. Even the sailors using a longboat could not row the vessel out of the current. "We have done everything that can be done," said the captain to Taylor. But Taylor replied, "No, there is one thing we have not done yet." There were three other believers on the ship, and Taylor suggested that each retire to his own cabin and pray for a breeze. They did, and while he was at prayer, Taylor received confidence from God that the desperately needed wind would be sent. He went up on deck and suggested to the first officer, an unbeliever, that he let down the mainsail because a breeze was on its way. The man refused, but then they saw the corner of the sail begin to stir. The breeze had come! They let down the sail and in a short time were on their way! (*A-Z Illustrations*)

In both of those cases – that of Taylor and of Daniel – **what was the secret to success?** It was not simply prayer, though that was included. It was not simply obedience, though that was included. **In each case, the men recognized their calling, and followed choices inside of that calling.**

Taylor's wind came after Taylor sought God (as the *Bible* instructed) and got assurance. Daniel's deferment came after he committed to do what God said in His Word. Both knew their call would only be significantly fulfilled by commitment – no matter what the outcome.

Compromise, when it comes to obedience to God's Word, is settling for less than our call. Keep your life goal – to honor

God with your days – at the center of your thinking when making even small life choices.

Rule 4: Don't get self-centered and believe you can create success alone. (1:9-10)

Remember, we serve God, not our own ability to manipulate situations. When we have what appears to be a "success," we must humbly remember it is God Who gave it to us. (1:9)

Your life is more than what you can accomplish – it is what God can do through you when you yield your members to Him. That is the excitement of following God! *"I can do all things through Christ Who strengthens me"*. (Phil. 4:13)

Look at Daniel 1:9:

Daniel 1:9 Now God granted Daniel favor and compassion in the sight of the commander of the officials.

Don't miss that Daniel wasn't arrogant, nor did he "command God" to do anything. He is God in Heaven, and I am a man on Earth – "let my words be few..." as Solomon long ago reminded. Later in this journal of God's work, Dan will face a lion's den. His friends will face a furnace of fire. Their delivery was not certain.

The point of our lives is not to obey for personal benefit – that is cloaked religious selfishness. Rather it **is to make much of Jesus** – and to honor our King! Our sacrifice is but a small thing if it will allow those who follow our time see His glory.

Self-centered Christianity sold well in the last thirty years. "Give a dollar so you can get ten" thinking was never about worship at its core. The favor Daniel received was by God's hand – but the opposite could have happened – and God would still be God. With every successful outreach, let us recall God's good hand;

with every painful setback let us seek God's path of direction. Self-centeredness is the antithesis of Christianity. He is the story: I am the messenger. He is the Lord, and I am His servant...period.

Rule 5: Be sympathetic to the other side without giving in on truth. (1:11-16)

Daniel knew how to listen with understanding to the fears of the ungodly around him (1:10). He tried his best to meet them halfway and still not compromise God's call (1:11-16). What did it hurt to try to live truth in an inoffensive way?

Daniel 1:10 ...and the commander of the officials said to Daniel, "I am afraid of my lord the king who has appointed your food and your drink; for why should he see your faces looking more haggard than the youths who are your own age? Then you would make me forfeit my head to the king." 11 But Daniel said to the overseer whom the commander of the officials had appointed over Daniel, Hananiah, Mishael and Azariah, 12 "Please test your servants for ten days, and let us be given some vegetables to eat and water to drink. 13 "Then let our appearance be observed in your presence and the appearance of the youths who are eating the king's choice food; and deal with your servants according to what you see." 14 So he listened to them in this matter and tested them for ten days. 15 At the end of ten days, their appearance seemed better and they were fatter than all the youths who had been eating the king's choice food. 16 So the overseer continued to withhold their choice food and the wine they were to drink, and kept giving them vegetables.

Some would criticize Dan for "compromising faith" because he wasn't belligerent and sarcastic in his commentary. They truly believe that any attempt to acknowledge what others are concerned about is a sign of weakness. Think for a moment: Is the strength of our argument for God IN the argument itself? I believe not. I believe it is found in seeking God. Our gentle reasonableness should not be read as weakness – but as confidence that from prayer and God's conviction in the hardest of hearts will come fruitful conversions where there would otherwise be none. No one is argued into the Kingdom of God. They are converted from within through prayer and God's Spirit pricking their heart. Sarcasm and argument may strengthen the soul of the discouraged believers, but prayer and God's conviction is what saves the unbeliever.

Let me ask you to do some things:

- Argue less and pray more.
- Wrestle less with the world in articles and news, and wrestle more for them on your knees.
- Don't panic over evil, fight back in Heavenly places.
- Don't feel the need to correct the world; just encourage, pray and look for an opportunity to show love to them.
- Stop the whining over lost men acting like lost men, and start the winning of souls by the power of the Cross.
- Stop being defensive and start being sympathetic to the plight of a dying world – they cannot help but spread death, all the while fearing it.

Doors will open that never have before. **The chief symbol of our faith was once a marker to the Roman world of their victory over Christ – a Cross. What does that tell you of our message? In our weakness, He will be shown unstoppably strong.**

Rule 6: Choose time with positive people and doing positive things. (1:17-19)

Look also at Daniel's companions. They were not alone, but together. They were learners, positively engaged and delightfully partnered with one another. People that are engaged in growth and life are invigorating and get better opportunities to be used of God (1:17-19).

Daniel 1:17 As for these four youths, God gave them knowledge and intelligence in every [branch of] literature and wisdom; Daniel even understood all [kinds of] visions and dreams. 18 Then at the end of the days, which the king had specified for presenting them, the commander of the officials presented them before Nebuchadnezzar. 19 The king talked with them, and out of them all not one was found like Daniel, Hananiah, Mishael and Azariah; so they entered the king's personal service.

Keep people, words, and activities that help you stay up in your sight! I love that simple saying in *Life's Little Instruction Book*: "Think big thoughts but relish small pleasures." (H. Jackson Brown, Jr.) The small-mindedness of Christians really grates against my soul... Can we speak of other things besides politics and culture wars? Is not the universe filled with God's fingerprints?

Don't worry; we will all get it wrong from time to time. That is why I like to recall the simple words of Oswald Avery: Whenever you fall, pick something up. Obviously, I am speaking of mistakes, not overlooking serious moral failures in ourselves. At the same time, just choose to be together with other believers. The world will get cold, but huddling can keep us warm. In our recharged warmth – we will be more ready to show the lost a way to the warmth. Cold, worn, dispirited believers bring no one to Christ, but usher many away from Him.

Rule 7: Work out your giftedness and stay at your post for God. (1:20-21)

The end of the chapter mentions the tenure of Dan. He was taken in 606, but stayed in the work until 537 – nearly 70 years later! He had God's hand in his life, but throughout the story, he learned to wait until God opened a door. Daniel 1 records:

Daniel 1:20 As for every matter of wisdom and understanding about which the king consulted them, he found them ten times better than all the magicians [and] conjurers who [were] in all his realm. 21 And Daniel continued until the first year of Cyrus the king.

Grabbing a headline and gaining a post are one thing – following through for seventy long years is yet another! Daniel watched a lot of bad legislation roll through during his tenure. He lived in a world of politics – a tough world in any age to be a decent man. He faced deceptions from enemies that fronted for the spiritual enemy – and we will watch how he navigated each challenge. Yet, he remained positive in the journey. He did it by refusing to be deceived with the others of his time. **Don't let the current circumstances of life convince you of the great deceptions of the enemy of your soul.**

- **He will try to deceive you about his strength.** In you, beloved follower of Jesus, is One greater than he who fluffs and puffs in this world.
- **He will try to discourage you by confusion.** For you, life events may hang like loose threads below a tapestry – but design is not discovered on this side of the cloth.
- **He will try to divert you with troubles.** Before you may be problems insurmountable for a time – but you were made for eternity.
- **He will try to dishearten you with memories.** Behind you, the call of old defeats may beckon to slow your progress – but your best days are ahead in the Father's house.

Since he is not greater, since your troubles last for but a season, since what is unknown now will become clear one day in the time after time, and since our Father has the power to forgive wholly and forget completely –**we must not allow the deception of the enemy to deter us from serving our King with an encouraged heart. Because life is filled with negative people and situations does not mean the believer should be negative.**

Shine the Light
Lessons in Daniel

Lesson Two: Daniel 2:1-23 "Six Positive Truths about Life's Problems"

It seems that everyone you know has problems – but some are overtaken by them. Listen to the people in your life. Each one has something going on that makes them uncomfortable. Some have MANY things in their lives that are difficult. Still others are inundated by life's troubles. Many people think their problem is as simple as "not having enough money" or "running out of time." When you talk to families, the problems they mention include "communication" or "boundary issues." When you talk to co-workers, they may tell you they "just need another job." When you get time with dear friends, – a couple you have known well – they may tell you of "intimacy issues." People will tell you of literally dozens of things they think would make them happy – if only they could change the conditions of their life.

Behaviorists and life coaches have assembled some of the problems they hear of most from their clients:

- **Dread:** Many of us live with a sense of foreboding about life. We are afraid we will not have enough money to make it through the month. We are afraid of some people because of unresolved issues in our past. We face new situations with such fear that we are often robbed of enjoying them. With each passing year, we have to work harder at keeping a sense of humor – because so many serious issues are raising uncertainty inside us.

- **Drift:** Many people feel like life is passing them by, and they aren't going anywhere. They want to make a difference somewhere, and to someone – but it just isn't happening.

- **Disgrace:** Some have deep feelings of worthlessness, or a sense that decisions they made in the past have left them with a deep stain deserving of punishment. They may feel they have an incurable flaw – and they are deeply sensitive to any kind of rejection.

- **Desolation:** Some people believe that no one loves them or truly cares about them. They feel alone in this world, as if their presence here matters little to anyone. Often this feeling follows the loss of a life partner sometime after they are alone. Though it is often temporary – it is a deep chasm of emotion.

- **Defensiveness:** Some have held old grudges and been bitter for a long time – and those old memories push out when they feel someone may hurt them. Some present themselves as victims – avoiding responsibility for their lives, while other recoil and strike almost without provocation. At the pace of life, many of us report that we have a tendency to respond too quickly to any perceived crisis – often without the tact we wish we would have had. We forget that under the pressures of the day, things can look worse and seem more intractably complex than they truly are. We fail to take the time to gain any real perspective.

- **Doubtfulness:** Some people so overthink their lives, they can barely live them. Inner reflection becomes stubborn inertia – and they "get stuck" in their own head.

After years of listening to people talk about their problems, I would like to offer a bold assertion. **I think I may know the single biggest problem each of us has – and it is the SAME problem for young and old, single and married, wealthy and poor.** It is the problem that acts as the lens to all other problems.

The biggest problem we have is HOW WE VIEW OUR PROBLEMS.

How a man or woman handles the adversity of life may be the best window into their true character. Under pressure, we show much of our true self. Can we see it differently?

Key Principle: Adversity can be another tool for shaping our lives in the hands of a creative God!

Today we continue with the story of four Hebrew men in a pagan culture. These young believers were yanked from their homes and dropped into a world that was foreign in every way– language, culture, and morality. They faced times of temptation, as well as times of peril. Our lesson today includes a record of what happened when they were forced to stare down the barrel of a gun that was sent for their collective executions – an excessive penalty because of others that failed at their task.

Daniel's life was in peril. The king he served had a dream and told his advisors to both recount the dream and interpret it, or face death by dismemberment. The ill-equipped counselors trembled and bartered for time. In a flash of temper, the king commanded mass executions be planned, and all the wise men of Babylon be gathered for the "culling of the intelligencia." News got to Daniel, when his "escort to execution" arrived, and he asked for time to seek God, along with his companions.

It occurs to me that Daniel could have been really discouraged that again he was facing difficulties that weren't directly related to his own failures. His captivity was a result of the failed kings of Judah, and the current threat was the result of a rash king surrounded by slippery godless counselors. <u>Yet, placing blame is wholly unhelpful when facing an imminent firing squad.</u> **What**

Daniel needed was God's help, or he would soon be visiting God's eternal home. Rather than grouse at God or blame his fellows – he dropped to his knees in humble request for compassion from Heaven.

Serious problems require a serious response – and there is none more serious than prayers offered while staring down the barrel of a gun. Fighting with God keeps us from falling before God – and that is where we belong when in trouble.

Why does God allow problems to assail His followers? Why doesn't He insulate them from the effects of the Fall of Man? **The truth is that times of trouble are often the most significant times for God to show Himself, and teach principles of truth about life we could never hear in the clatter of peace, prosperity and success.**

Let's look at **six truths we can grasp when times of trouble rush in upon us:**

Truth 1: Moments of trouble are one of God's chief times of uncovering great truths. (2:1)

Daniel 2:1 Now in the second year of the reign of Nebuchadnezzar, Nebuchadnezzar had dreams; and his spirit was troubled and his sleep left him.
Before we dig into verse one, did you notice the term "second year"? Since we know from Daniel 1:5 and 1:18 that Daniel and his friends were already on a three-year course, and we see in Daniel 2:13-14 that he appears to have graduated – the term "second year" can pose a problem.

There are essentially two possibilities:
- **First,** Daniel was named a "wise man" with his friends while he was still in training. That is not as likely as the second idea.

- **Second,** Nebuchadnezzar served for several years under his father Nabopolassar. Once he defeated the Assyrians and their Egyptian allied armies, Nabopolassar turned the throne to his son, Nebuchadnezzar II. Within months of his abdication in 605 BCE, Nabopolassar died of natural causes aged about 53 years. It could be the point of the timing was the second year of the SOLE REIGN of Nebuchadnezzar – or about 604 BCE. One ancient source, a Chaldean historian named Berosus (only now available through other extant sources) stated that Nabopolassar was aged and infirm, and gave up a part of his army to his son Nebuchadnezzar, who defeated the Egyptian host at Carchemish on the Euphrates, and also drove Pharaoh Necho out of Asia. Nebuchadnezzar then marched to Jerusalem and Jehoiakim surrendered to him – the beginning of the seventy years of Babylonian, captivity.

Here is the point of the record of the dream in Scripture... What looks like LIFE-DRIVING FORCES aren't just a series of coincidental events – it is the work of a providential God! **Difficulty is often God's hand at work shaping His people –** sometimes even through the enemy's powerful plans to defeat them! **What the enemy means for one's destruction – God can use for their good.**

Stand in the throne room of Nebuchadnezzar the morning after he roused from half-sleep, grumpy because of his fitful nightmarish restlessness. He was being pushed around by forces stronger than he was, and being a great king wasn't insulating him from discomfort.

Don't forget that even celebrities, millionaires, and presidents can have toothaches. No one is truly in control of life this side of Heaven, no matter how much he thinks he is. One tiny piece of lead changed a presidency when I was a child. It was a tragedy,

but it reminded the whole country that NO ONE is able to control everything! The king was being pushed by a problem.
Here is the truth: You can be pushed by problems or led by God – it all comes down to your choice of Whom or what to follow in life.

While it is true that we must NOT lay our problems passively at another's feet - but address them and take responsibility for them… it is also equally true that we must have the humility and honesty to recognize that we do not truly control the Earth we live on, or the body we live within.

Look up. You didn't hang the stars… One of the truly startling things about the naturalists that pervade in our time is their utter arrogance. They speak boldly – as if the sciences are so thoroughly true and the research is so absolutely consistent. What will shake even the most secular man or woman's confidence in that arrogance is to look closely enough at the tons of research – only to discover how utterly inadequate we are to discern truth. The king was complaining, and God was simply making a point and creating a drama to display Himself to a man who THOUGHT he was in charge of the world.

Truth 2: Problems force an unbeliever to use the system they created without God. (2:2)

Daniel 2:2 Then the king gave orders to call in the magicians, the conjurers, the sorcerers and the Chaldeans to tell the king his dreams. So they came in and stood before the king.

Look at the kinds of EXPERTS that were on the payroll of the king:

- There were the **magicians** (*khar-tome'*: a horoscope reader; as in drawing magical lines or circles). This is someone that reads the world to find answers in the cosmos – a more modern version of superstitious animism. "The universe knows" is their mantra.

- Then there were the **conjurers** (*ash-shawf'*: a necromancer or exorcist). This is someone who claims to be able to breach at will the veil between the physical and spiritual world and speak to those beyond the veil (the dead). They use as evidence the ability to hypnotize to persuade people, snakes, etc.

- Next, there were the **sorcerers** (a rendering of the Hebrew *mekhashphim*: literally, mutterers, men who professed to have power with evil spirits. From *kaw-shaf'*: to whisper a spell, enchant or practice magic or witchcraft). In the *Bible*, some of the harshest punishments are given to them, as they claim to direct the spirits of the enemy of the Lord and His people.

- Finally, there were the **Chaldeans** (*kas-dee'*: literally the inhabitants of Chaldea, with a long tradition of wise sayings and formulas). These are the imported experts from think tanks with interesting pedigrees.

These men were educated by the world's standards. **They were degree-carrying professors that were FULL OF THEMSELVES.** Later, we will note Daniel's reaction – which was startlingly humble. He was their total opposite. Lost man looks within.

Believers know that anything in there is already broken – so they get direction from the Word and in prayer – because the answer is not within. Beyond the Word hidden within (and that is subject to a fading memory) and the Spirit prompting (and that needs to be checked against the Word) – there is little in myself that I can truly trust.

The more educated a man or woman becomes, often the less dogmatic they are about the field in which they were educated.

Do you know why? The answer is this: <u>The best process for learning will inevitably reveal how weak and flawed we are. It is harder to trust ourselves when we see how much the research led us to the wrong conclusions in the past.</u> **Don't fear education – despise the indoctrination that is attempting to pass as education. Real education begins with the knowledge that we aren't the standard – because the reverence of the Lord is the beginning of wisdom.** The *Bible* calls those who do not believe in God by the simple term: "fool." Consider this: when a fool attempts to make others into fools – the result is not real education at all – it is foolish indoctrination with hellish result.

Truth 3: Problems reveal the hopeless cynicism that lurks beneath the surface of the unbelieving world. (2:3-9)

There is an old English saying: "There is no honor among thieves". It points to the problem of building a life surrounded by people with little character. The king of Babylon had such a life...

Daniel 2:3 The king said to them, "I had a dream and my spirit is anxious to understand the dream." 4 Then the Chaldeans spoke to the king in Aramaic: "O king, live forever! Tell the dream to your servants, and we will declare the interpretation." 5 The king replied to the Chaldeans, "The command from me is firm: if you do not make known to me the dream and its interpretation, you will be torn limb from limb and your houses will be made a rubbish heap. 6 "But if you declare the dream and its interpretation, you will receive from me gifts and a reward and great honor; therefore declare to me the dream and its interpretation." 7 They answered a second time and said, "Let the king tell the dream to his servants, and we will declare the interpretation." 8 The king replied, "I know for certain that you are bargaining for time, inasmuch as you have seen that the command from me is firm, 9 that if you do not make the dream known to me, there is only one decree for you. For you have agreed together to speak lying and corrupt words before me until the situation is changed; therefore tell me the dream, that I may know that you can declare to me its interpretation."

The king made clear several times EXACTLY what he wanted. The advisors did all they could to move his firm pronouncement, but the king was stuck on his plan. You have to sympathize with the advisors – even if you don't like them! There is nothing as dark as recognizing you have met your own end and you are powerless to stop the events that are leading you to it.

Someone has said, Problems seem most acute when we spend an inordinate time trying to do something about things we can't do anything about. Isn't that a word for our time? Each day we tune into news about a world that seems spinning out of control. It isn't, but because it isn't in OUR control, it can feel that way. That is why I find comfort at my heavenly Father's feet.

I must be honest with you. If your fulfillment and happiness is dependent upon other people – you had better be sure they are flawless people that cannot and will not turn to selfishness – or you are in deep trouble. I highly recommend you consider placing your full trust in an unchanging God revealed in the Scriptures. My experience has taught me that people are unreliable. My *Bible* has made clear that my experience is not unique.

The king should have consulted a good football coach like Lou Holtz of yesteryear. He said, Don't tell your problems to people: eighty percent don't care; and the other twenty percent are glad you have them. (Lou Holtz quotes *American Football Coach*, 1937-1980).

The advisors were stuck, not just by the size of the task, but also by the disbelief of the king. He knew they messed with him to tell him what they wanted him to hear. You can tolerate "apple polishers" and sycophants when times are good, but when serious and painful issues arise, you must have around you trusted souls, – and they are few and far between.

Truth 4: Problems expose the limits of experts without relationship to their Creator. (2:10)

The room was filled with EXPERTS but not with any people who knew God. The elaborate costumes and pageantry could do little in the face of a task that required a certain and reliable link to the spiritual world. Daniel's journal continued:

Daniel 2:10 The Chaldeans answered the king and said, "There is not a man on Earth who could declare the matter for the king, inasmuch as no great king or ruler has [ever] asked anything like this of any magician, conjurer or Chaldean. 11 Moreover, the thing which the king demands is difficult, and there is no one else who could declare it to the king except gods, whose dwelling place is not with [mortal] flesh."

The next time you hear of "men of science" proving things that are beyond their ability, bear in mind the futility of their quest. If there really is a God in Heaven as the *Bible* teaches, and there really are one quintillion stars as astronomers estimate, and there really are literally billions of planets spinning in millions of solar systems, what is the likelihood that a guy in California has the skills and ability to put his mind around all that and come to the conclusion of how it works?

Let me take this argument from naturalists that are pressing on us. One author stated:

"Let's agree that there is no empirical evidence showing that God exists. If you think about it as a rational person, this lack of evidence is startling. There is not one bit of empirical evidence indicating that today's "God," nor any other contemporary god, nor any god of the past, exists. In addition, we know that:

- If we had scientific proof of God's existence, we would talk about the "science of God" rather than "faith in God."

- If we had scientific proof of God's existence, the study of God would be a scientific endeavor rather than a theological one.

- If we had scientific proof of God's existence, all religious people would be aligning on the God that had been scientifically proven to exist. Instead, there are thousands of gods and religions.

The reason for this lack of evidence is easy for any unbiased observer to see. The reason why there is no empirical evidence for God is because God is imaginary." (Cut from the website "www.godisimaginary.com").

Hmm. Look at the sheer **arrogance** of the person making such claims.

- Their claim is that there is **no empirical evidence for God's existence**. The *Bible* answers simply: "Look up! The organization of the **cosmos is not a random phenomenon** – but bears every resemblance of a design carefully executed by an intelligent Creator."

- Their claim is that **because they don't call God's existence a "science" but rather "faith," He doesn't exist.** The *Bible*'s claim is simple: **The world can make any definitions and claims they like – that doesn't make their limited observations into absolute truths.**

- Their claim is that if there was scientific evidence for God, the study of God would be in the field of scientific endeavor, not to a limited study of theology.

Look into history that is bigger than the back of a cereal box. For centuries, people like the scientist Isaac Newton – the professor of physics - practiced the craft for EXACTLY the purpose of exposing truths about the Creator.

In fact, naturalists deliberately drive teachers that want to do so **out of state schools** and then have the audacity to **use that as proof that science must somehow disprove God**. That is like a board of education removing all references to a former President from textbooks and then using the textbooks to prove the guy never held the office!

Here is my point: George Bernard Shaw was right when he wrote, **Science... never solves a problem without creating ten more**. It isn't because they aren't trying; it is because **they have a limit to what they can observe**, and limited minds to do the observation.

Go back to the throne room where Nebuchadnezzar just unloaded on these experts. Note the list of people that were invited and their claims that they could pierce the spiritual world. Why were they now claiming, when placed under the hot lights, that they had no such power (see "whose dwelling place is not with mortal flesh")!

When all is said and done – men who claim to know the reaches of eternity from looking into a test tube are overselling their ability. Science can observe some phenomena and help explain some processes – but it cannot see the edges of all that exists, and it cannot explain WHY it exists – that is beyond the ability of man. Only arrogant men claim to know what they cannot know – but sensible people know they are overstating their knowledge.

Truth 5: Problems create a platform for the clear presentation of God's ability to fix life. (2:12-16)

Can I ask you to see a truth that can potentially change the way you look at tomorrow's hassles? **Consider how every problem is a platform for God to show YOU something, and show OTHERS something through your life.**

At this point in our story, enter a quiet, unassuming and godly man named Dan...

Daniel 2:12 Because of this the king became indignant and very furious and gave orders to destroy all the wise men of Babylon. 13 So the decree went forth that the wise men should be slain; and they looked for Daniel and his friends to kill [them]. 14 Then Daniel replied with discretion and discernment to Arioch, the captain of the king's bodyguard, who had gone forth to slay the wise men of Babylon; 15 he said to Arioch, the king's commander, "For what reason is the decree from the king [so] urgent?" Then Arioch informed Daniel about the matter. 16 So Daniel went in and requested of the king that he would give him time, in order that he might declare the interpretation to the king.

Daniel heard about the problem after the experts had left the throne room and went home to write their respective "Last Will and Testaments" and kiss their kids goodbye... Watch closely how Daniel responded to the man who brought the news.

- First, Daniel measured the rank of the man with whom he was speaking, and spoke with the discernment of both the situation and the man. He didn't use bluster, but asked and listened.

- Second, he used a form of the word *ta'am* – the word for TASTE. He tactfully, tastefully, politely, but directly asked what situation caused this turn of events.

Daniel recognized that HE couldn't solve the problem, but he knew GOD COULD. He shared with the lost king that if he asked, God COULD make all of it known. He asked for time to see if God WOULD fill the need. (2:16)

By now, some *Bible* students are inwardly asking a question: "Why did the king let Daniel have time when he was so pushy with the other so-called experts?" I think the issue came down to ONE THING - track record.

Daniel got the benefit of the doubt because Daniel hadn't tried to personally gain favor from the king in any way. He didn't use the perks and powers given him to anxiously get MORE PERKS AND POWERS. The king was no idiot. He was a seasoned veteran of one of the world's largest armies. He was groomed for the task of leadership by a father who was very successful in his own right. The king was a fine judge of character, and knew that Daniel wasn't blowing smoke up his royal tunic.

Now focus your eyes on Daniel. The believer isn't in the business of using God's power to gain power or prestige for himself. A godly man must proceed with caution and wait on God to succeed… or in this case meet God face to face because God didn't speak.

Daniel didn't need to panic, he needed to pray and seek God's face for important news. If God chose to solve the problem – the testimony of the Lord would grow. If He did not choose to speak, Daniel would have little unconfessed since the next event in his life would be his last event. In many ways, our problems are God's opportunity to preach through the sermon of our lives.

Truth 6: Problems give an opportunity to draw us to each other, and eventually to worship and praise of our God! (2:17-23)

Our account of Daniel's last meeting with his friends before God broke into the story is found in the next few verses. This prayer meeting was as focused as any you will ever experience. No one slept through it. No one let his mind wander. No one was focused on the temperature of the room, the comfort of the chairs or the eloquence of the praying partner. This was a meeting with God – and there is nothing else like it on Earth…

Daniel 2:17 Then Daniel went to his house and informed his friends, Hananiah, Mishael and Azariah, about the matter, 18 so that they might request compassion from the God of Heaven concerning this mystery, so that Daniel and his friends would not be destroyed with the rest of the wise men of Babylon. 19 Then the mystery was revealed to Daniel in a night vision. Then Daniel blessed the God of Heaven…

God answered the prayers of the men. He didn't HAVE TO, but He CHOSE to do so. Daniel got the answer in the same night air that brought the problem to the king in the first place. What he did NEXT reveals what he was INSIDE…

Daniel 2:20 Daniel said, "Let the name of God be blessed forever and ever, for wisdom and power belong to Him. 21 It is He Who changes the times and the epochs; He removes kings and establishes kings; He gives wisdom to wise men and knowledge to men of understanding. 22 It is He Who reveals the profound and hidden things; He knows what is in the darkness, and the light dwells with Him. 23 To You, O God of my fathers, I give thanks and praise, for You have given me wisdom and power; even now You have made known to me what we requested of You, for You have made known to us the king's matter."
Daniel worshiped and praised God with some choice words about His wonders.

- God sets up kingdoms and takes them down at will. It isn't up to the UN, the Congress or the World Court –

God can dry up an ocean, or flood a desert. He is unstoppable!

- God can raise up a man or woman to the highest position among their peers – and can just as easily recall them to the dust of the ground. The author of life can place a period in any life He chooses, on any page He chooses.

- God can expose the darkest, shadowed truths – forcing them to roll out into the light. Men become wise by listening and following His Word – humbly, openly and honestly. There is no truth in any other, and there is no knowledge that can be gained apart from Him! Reverence for HIM is the beginning of knowledge.

- God sees what no one else can – period. He has the answer before we have the question – because the answer is found inside of His character. He alone can fulfill, and He alone can truly explain.

Can we not see it clearly? God uses our troubles as His megaphone to a world adrift – but only if we stop fussing at Him and start following Him. Small troubles can build our strength and toughness, while great troubles can offer us a platform from which God can speak. Old troubles can soften us to be an encourager to weaker ones about us – as they pass through the conditioning of their own struggles.

It is true... **Adversity can be another tool for shaping our lives in the hands of a Creative God!**

Remember these four things:
- We must not **run** from trouble, but **face** it squarely.
- We are n**ot big enough** to handle it, but **God** is – and we don't have to do it alone.
- The "all things" a believer can do "through Christ that strengthens him" includes whatever problem you may be facing today.Snow White was right, "**Someday my Prince WILL come!**"

Shine the Light
Lessons in Daniel

(Note: The book of Daniel is twelve chapters, with Daniel 1-6 a biographical and historical narrative, with the exception on 2:19-45, and Daniel 7-12 a series of prophetic records. Daniel 2:19-45 is Lesson Seven as the beginning of the prophetic part of the book.)

Lesson Three: Daniel 3:1-30 "The Puppet Masters"

Over the past few weeks, when I get a few minutes for entertainment reading, I have been pouring over Dan Brown's book *Inferno*, a fascinating story set in Florence, Italy – the city famous for the home of Dante Alighieri, the famous poet author from the dawn of the fourteenth century. Dan Brown is a good storyteller, which is evidenced by the popularity of one release after another. I am only a third of the way through this book, but I admit the plot does grab you, and thrust you into the fictional story. The characters seem quite believable. I won't take the time to explain his tale, except to say that the premise of the book is that there is a shadow organization that is at work behind many seemingly unconnected events on the international stage, working for clients that have their own agenda. What would appear to be a car accident in one country, and a boating accident a month later in another – were actually connected plots that would take enormous effort to detect – and that was by design.

I admit that I am not a conspiracy theorist by nature. I tend to be a skeptic about many of these "so-called plots" that swirl around. Yet, I do believe that behind men and women of power, a case can be made that other forces are at work – and perhaps those forces are more organized than I have been able to grasp. I don't know – the world is a big place, and I am not knowledgeable enough to conclude much about sweeping agendas and powerful strings.

At the same time, when I look back into God's Word, I find a story that reads like one of Dan Brown's plot lines. The one I want to consider in this lesson is taken from a journal preserved from the sixth century BCE, written by a Babylonian sage who was also named Daniel. His story is so compelling that I would bet Dan Brown would buy this book himself, and his story wasn't fiction. Let me set the scene:

The room was dark and the shadows many. The men who gathered there treasured darkness, because the words they spoke meant pain, trouble and sometimes even death to those touched by their evil sway. They didn't want fame – men like these prefer not to be known and celebrated publicly. These are men behind the political scene. They didn't want to be interviewed on the Sunday morning talk shows from the capitol. These men wanted something much, much more valuable... they wanted power over decision makers. These faceless king-makers made sure every word uttered was carefully measured – because power must be carefully guarded if it is to be maintained. They spoke slowly of detail and of plots unfolding in a world that had literally no suspicion at all of the strings of their puppet masters. These political architects carefully wove a plan from three powerful strands. They used the zeal of misplaced religious fervor – for little is as powerful and as adaptable. They blended their plot with a dose of political intrigue and then folded in the basest impulse of all – the pure unbridled arrogance of self-promoting politicians. None of the plotters looked much past their own advancement. They cared little for the lofty goals of civil morality or kingdom longevity – what they craved was growing influence that led to their utter dominance...and they would do whatever it took to secure their place of power.

That is the story Daniel unfolds in chapter three. This time, he isn't relating his own experience, but rather the **experience of three friends that were snatched away from Judah at the same time he was brought to Babylon**. Daniel made plain that a king was sucked in by his own ego to making proclamations that hurt believers. Ruthless political players brought persecution down on the heads of believers that put the future of the message of God in Babylon in peril.

Yet, the passage isn't about the problem – it NEVER is. **It is about the POWER of God and the confidence we can have in Him!**

Last time I tried to convince you that the greatest problem most of us have is the way we VIEW our problems. As I open to chapter three, I am deliberately bypassing the last part of Daniel 2, because I will be handling the prophecy portions of Daniel in detail in a future lesson. I want to continue to press the issue of HOW WE VIEW TROUBLE, because this book addresses it with precision. Chapter Three unfolds a principle that I believe is significant…

Key Principle: Dark times are unique opportunities for piercing light to make a real difference!

Drop into the story of an ancient king who has been reading the mail of sycophants and flatterers and decided on a building project that he thought was a suitable self-tribute:

Daniel 3:1 Nebuchadnezzar the king made an image of gold, the height of which [was] sixty cubits (ninety feet tall) [and] its width six cubits (nine feet wide); he set it up on the plain of Dura in the province of Babylon.

The entire story can be divided into two simple parts – nothing fancier is needed! The **first part is the <u>development of the</u>**

problem, and the **second part is the response of the believer**.

The Problem Developed: (Daniel 3:1-15)

Set-up: The enemy of God and his people often uses a familiar cocktail recipe:

First, he misdirected a man of power and influence – in this case the king of one of the great superpowers of the world. Satan's most effective work begins with the soft blowing of subtle influence pushing along a fragile ego. Think of it: Nebuchadnezzar was the undisputed king of perhaps the world's most elegant city and most powerful government – and yet he thought what was truly lacking in his kingdom was a ninety-foot tall statue of himself. His most pressing issue wasn't health care, not education, not immigration, not civil rights; he concluded his biggest problem that needed the most serious investment – was his image sculpting. Only one who is thoroughly self-absorbed could draw such a conclusion. **When a leader becomes more consumed with image than effect, he has lost his way, and the breath of the enemy has become a driving wind.**

Second, he confused the man with religious symbolism – the image of Nebuchadnezzar's dream from chapter two. (He dreamed of a great statue and the prophet Daniel explained that Nebuchadnezzar played a direct role in the interpretation of its meaning.) The image was a statue, and the king got the idea from misguided religious thought that he should build one of himself. **Bad theology leads to bad action, but is most often driven by good impulse.** How many times has a social program been started by a leader who wanted to help? – But his solution actually added many unintended consequences that hurt more than were aided.

Third, ego produced paganism (the celebration of the creation over the Creator), **which in turn produced persecution.**

Clearly, the meaning of the dream of rising and falling kingdoms was disclosed by God as something that came from HIM – but the arrogance of the king caused him to dismiss the real lesson – that God is in control of the rise and fall of kingdoms. **Dismissal of truth is the beginning of the adoption of error.**

Daniel sets the scene well in Daniel 3:1. Here is the truth: The prophet described the scene in detail, as men erected a ninety-foot tall statue of their leader for all to see. He understood the OPPORTUNITY of the problem of this new brand of enforced paganism... Powerful people may behave badly and lead with what seems like unending ego, but that doesn't change the people of God and their mission, or their passion to follow God and love people... Don't stop reading Daniel's account after he details the statue – or you are left with only the problem. That is what the NEWS MEDIA does. It leads you to the intractable issues of our day, and offers the blur of contradictory opinions of pundits from opposite sides of the aisle. God's Word isn't about the problem. It is about the platform the problem affords the believer to shine a light on that pierces the darkness. That is how it unfolds answers.

Surge: In the face of the enemy at work – the wave of compliance by godless men looks overwhelming!

Daniel 3:2 Then Nebuchadnezzar the king sent [word] to assemble the satraps, the prefects and the governors, the counselors, the treasurers, the judges, the magistrates and all the rulers of the provinces to come to the dedication of the image that Nebuchadnezzar the king had set up. 3 Then the satraps, the prefects and the governors, the counselors, the treasurers, the judges, the magistrates and all the rulers of the provinces were assembled for the dedication of the image that Nebuchadnezzar the king had set up; and they stood before the image that Nebuchadnezzar had set up. 4 Then the herald loudly proclaimed: "To you the command is given, O peoples, nations and [men of every] language, 5 that at the moment you hear the sound of the horn, flute, lyre, trigon, psaltery, bagpipe and all kinds of music, you are to fall down and worship the golden image that Nebuchadnezzar the king has set up. 6 "But whoever does not fall down and worship shall immediately be cast into the midst of a furnace of blazing fire." 7 Therefore at that time, when all the peoples heard the sound of the horn, flute, lyre, trigon, psaltery, bagpipe and all kinds of music, all the peoples, nations and [men of every] language fell down [and] worshiped the golden image that Nebuchadnezzar the king had set up.

One of the most startling observations is that darkness can spread at such an alarming rate, with seemingly no obstacle to repulse the dark wave (3:2-7). It is in the face of the tsunami of evil the believer must be calm, and recall that although the conditions may be darkening, that doesn't change the people of God and their passion to follow God and love people. God doesn't allow evil to march forward without a purpose in the telling of His story. <u>The dark setting offers a rich backdrop for light to shine. Witness in dark times is much more profound.</u> No one likes to be hungry, but the joy of a full stomach is all the sweeter if hunger has been experienced – and vanquished.

Break down the verses, and **three ideas emerge:**

First, there was a **command**: Someone takes the lead in sponsoring darkness. In this case, word was spread and the powerful came to dedication (3:2-3). False ideas when presented with the power and symbolism of official channels often gains traction quickly. It is not by mistake that our government tests some social theory in the military – because opposition is slight in a chain of command situation.

Second, there were **conditions**: The announcement set clear expectation (3:4-6). A surge like this asserts MIND CONTROL. The king didn't want allegiance – he wanted worship. He wanted surrender to his will. Evil men cannot tolerate opposition, despite their claim that they are the tolerant ones among us. They don't want pagan ideas merely installed in our education system – they want unqualified control of our society's worldview. We resist because we know what they want. It isn't the freedom to live the way they choose – it is the right to force us to agree with them or be removed from the public square. If you doubt that, just become a celebrity and proclaim yourself for "traditional marriage." You won't have to condemn anyone. You won't need to say one negative word. The vilification will be swift and angry – offered by the voices that advocate "tolerance." It is a rouse, and honest people know it. <u>We must seek to be peaceable and kind, but never passive in defense of truth.</u>

Third, there was almost uniform **conformity**: People fell down in obedience with practically no resistance (3:7). We must remember that the **moral system of most people allows them to compromise anything to get ahead with those in power.** Believers don't have that luxury, because we serve the King above the king. That is now persecution typically developed in history. <u>The enemy positioned the authorities in such a way that believers could not choose to follow – thereby making them look like the divisive dissidents.</u>

That truth is not a reason for despair – it is a reason for us to live with CLARITY the principles of our Father in Heaven. As the backdrop color of the public square grows in contrast to biblical values, the people of God stand out more....Consider how profound it will look to have a deeply committed and happy marriage (as defined in the *Bible*) in the average workplace. These dark days offer us real OPPORTUNITY!

Squeezing: Anger and rage will be vented on any who question the rising evil.

Along with the set-up of the enemy and the surge of the crowd, there is one more feature that we observe as the dark clouds of trouble gather for a follower of God. It is the deliberate SQUEEZING of God's people. Watch how it happened in the story…

Daniel 3:8 For this reason at that time certain Chaldeans came forward and brought charges against the Jews. 9 They responded and said to Nebuchadnezzar the king, "O king, live forever! 10 You, O king, have made a decree that every man who hears the sound of the horn, flute, lyre, trigon, psaltery, and bagpipe, and all kinds of music is to fall down and worship the golden image. 11 But whoever does not fall down and worship shall be cast into the midst of a furnace of blazing fire. 12 There are certain Jews whom you have appointed over the administration of the province of Babylon, [namely] Shadrach, Meshach and Abed-nego. These men, O king, have disregarded you; they do not serve your gods or worship the golden image which you have set up."

The issue is about one thing… **control**: The enemy will use the dark days to try to wipe out God's message and messengers (3:8-12). He may even use those who were respectful and helpful just a short time before.

Look closely. What happened to these three Hebrews was out of their CONTROL. They hadn't done anything wrong. God wasn't punishing them for something they had done. SOMETIMES, things happen to us, which are beyond our CONTROL. It's not our fault. In those moments, remember that LIFE IS IN GOD'S CONTROL – not the control of godless men! When we despair at the wickedness, we blunt the knowledge of God's sovereignty! We can spend our time trying to find who is to blame, or trying to discern what God wants us to produce in the face of the problem.

- The **believers were not trying to be in the way**, but they attracted the ire of the Chaldeans. Jealous of their independence, the Chaldeans raised an accusation (3:8).

- The **unbelieving leaders appeared to have an "in" with the king**, and used that to set up persecution cloaked as a necessary nationalism and public good. (3:9-11).

- The **unbelievers framed the intent of the believers as hostile** to the power of the state. (3:12). This is the truth: Lying about the believer's intentions is not a new ploy – but a tried and true strategy. Rather than be appalled, we need to be prepared to stand up to false worship, as well as be prepared to address positively why we do what we do.

The squeeze became obvious as the king had the offenders dragged in:

Daniel 3:13 Then Nebuchadnezzar in rage and anger gave orders to bring Shadrach, Meshach and Abed-nego; then these men were brought before the king. 14 Nebuchadnezzar responded and said to them, "Is it true, Shadrach, Meshach, and Abed-nego that you do not serve my gods or worship the golden image that I have set up? 15 Now, if you are ready, at the moment you hear the sound of the horn, flute, lyre, trigon, psaltery and bagpipe and all kinds of music, to fall down and worship the image that I have made, [very well]. But if you do not worship, you will immediately be cast into the midst of a furnace of blazing fire; and what god is there who can deliver you out of my hands?"

Faced with a choice from which there was clearly no escape – the faith of three men became crystal clear. **This is the point of the problem – God wanted to show something to the king, and he chose to do it through the lives of these three men.**

The Believers Responded: (Daniel 3:16-30)

Contest: First, they faced the challenge – Put God above self. (3:13-15)

Look at the king's question! "But if you do not worship, you will immediately be cast into the midst of a furnace of blazing fire; and what god is there who can deliver you out of my hands?"
He had no idea there is an affirmative answer to the idea that there was a God Who could save them from his authority… and he was completely WRONG! **Believer, don't confuse confident assertion with certain truth.** The king may have believed he was in charge of all things, but that only lasted until the truth came out in FIRE. Fortunately, for him, it was a furnace. For others it will be a forever fire that is not quenched that will show them the truth.

Be careful with whom you pick a fight. The king not only CHALLENGED God when he set up the image for all to worship him … he CHALLENGED God for His ability to do anything about it. Nebuchadnezzar was on very dangerous ground.

Here is a truth that may not be popular – but we must grasp it: God may decide to offer YOU or ME – our lives – to win another to Himself. Ask any missionary if that is easy. If he is honest, he will tell you it is not. God has the right, and God knows the plan. Is it not a deep privilege to be used by the Creator to bring salvation to others? The contest is within the believer, but the conditions that make it clear are often in the world around him or her. The furnace and the throne became the platform for a clear testimony – as tough as it was to face it.

Confidence: (3:16-18) **They didn't need to rethink the issue because they knew the king's King!**

Don't forget: The enemy has every interest in dragging out and dramatizing his power – the power over your body. It is a temporal power, but it is all that he has to work with! The king offered another opportunity for the men to "bail" – a dragging out of the decision process, but the men would have no part in that.

Daniel 3:16 Shadrach, Meshach and Abed-nego replied to the king, "O Nebuchadnezzar, we do not need to give you an answer concerning this matter. 17 If it be [so], our God whom we serve is able to deliver us from the furnace of blazing fire; and He will deliver us out of your hand, O king. 18But [even] if [He does] not, let it be known to you, O king, that we are not going to serve your gods or worship the golden image that you have set up."

Can you pick out the confidence in these men? When we truly encounter God, we aren't nearly as impressed with human power, accomplishment and ability! Temporal power pales before eternal. That is why a biblical worldview is so critical... it will provide a foundation under the choices of our lives. If God is really in control, the enemy has a limitation on me. Whatever passes into my life, passes the approval of God's hand before it arrives to me.

Consider this: A submarine has enormous pressure on the hull as it sinks deeply in the ocean. It is only the inner counter pressure of the air that stops the outer pressure from collapsing the vessel into itself. For the same reason, – the world is trying to shape you into its image ... shape you into its mold. We aren't to be shaped by OUTSIDE forces - BUT - by the INSIDE strength and domination of the Holy Spirit. When you surrender to God's power and allow the work of the Spirit to take over within, you protect against collapse to the outer pressure to conform!

We cannot deny that part of what shapes us is the outer force as well. With no resistance, believers become weak and unchallenged.

In their book, *We Let Our Son Die*, Larry and Lucy Parker recount the tragic story of a misguided faith. In painful and painstaking detail, Larry and his wife paint the picture of how they had come to believe that if they just had enough faith, God would heal their diabetic son. Eventually, their son Wesley got ill and needed insulin. Believing that God would heal Wesley, they withheld the insulin and, predictably, Wesley lapsed into a diabetic coma. The Parkers, warned by some about the impropriety of not having enough faith, believed that God would heal Wesley. Unfortunately, Wesley died. But even after Wesley's death, the Parkers, undaunted in their "faith," conducted a resurrection service rather than a funeral service. In fact, for more than a year following his death, they refused to abandon their firmly held faith that Wesley, like Jesus, would rise from the dead. Eventually, both Larry and Lucy were tried and convicted of manslaughter and child abuse.

Isn't that a tragic story? Yes. But even more tragic, is that countless other stories with a flawed concept of faith inevitably leads to shipwreck—sometimes spiritually, in other cases physically, and in still other scenarios, both. Many Christians believe that the *Bible* teaches that faith is confidence in a certain outcome.

In our text, **they did not pretend to know what was going to happen to them**. These words may trouble you. Perhaps you want to say, "Oh, no, Shadrach, Meshach, and Abednego! No ifs, ands, or buts. Believe without doubting." However, these men did not operate on today's popular notion of what faith should be. Theirs was a biblical faith. God will do what He chooses, not what I choose. I control nothing, but He never leaves me in the process.

Companionship: By becoming servants like Jesus, they shared time with Him!

Watch the story finish with testimony:

Daniel 3:19 Then Nebuchadnezzar was filled with wrath, and his facial expression was altered toward Shadrach, Meshach and Abed-nego. He answered by giving orders to heat the furnace seven times more than it was usually heated. 20 He commanded certain valiant warriors who [were] in his army to tie up Shadrach, Meshach and Abed-nego in order to cast [them] into the furnace of blazing fire. ... 24 Then Nebuchadnezzar the king was astounded and stood up in haste; he said to his high officials, "Was it not three men we cast bound into the midst of the fire?" They replied to the king, "Certainly, O king." 25 He said, "Look! I see four men loosed [and] walking [about] in the midst of the fire without harm, and the appearance of the fourth is like a son of [the] gods!" 26 Then Nebuchadnezzar came near to the door of the furnace of blazing fire; he responded and said, "Shadrach, Meshach and Abed-nego, come out, you servants of the Most High God, and come here!" Then Shadrach, Meshach and Abed-nego came out of the midst of the fire. 27 The satraps, the prefects, the governors and the king's high officials gathered around [and] saw in regard to these men that the fire had no effect on the bodies of these men nor was the hair of their head singed, nor were their trousers damaged, nor had the smell of fire [even] come upon them. 28 Nebuchadnezzar responded and said, "Blessed be the God of Shadrach, Meshach and Abed-nego, who has sent His angel and delivered His servants who put their trust in Him, violating the king's command, and yielded up their bodies so as not to serve or worship any god except their own God. 29 "Therefore I make a decree that any people, nation or tongue that speaks anything offensive against the God of Shadrach, Meshach and Abed-nego shall be torn limb from limb and their houses reduced to a rubbish heap, inasmuch as there is no other god who is able to deliver in this way." 30 Then the king caused Shadrach, Meshach and Abed-nego to prosper in the province of Babylon.

Three men were hurled into a fiery furnace, but One was already in the fire waiting for them to arrive. The powerful men of the world stood outside in awe, while the King of the Ages had a little "pep talk" time with His faithful friends. In time, the men walked out of that furnace and showed the power of the God they served. **All this happened because they completely understood, and lived out one essential truth: Their lives were not their own. Their troubles were nothing less than God's platform to use each of them to speak to others.**

Every believer must face that difficult lesson… We aren't always going to be protected from troubles, but **we do get two opportunities**.

First, with trouble we are given an opportunity to display God's love and power.

Second, in the fire of trouble God draws nearer to us that we have ever known before!

Let's say it plainly: When we fear the fire more than God – we become ineffective and uncertain in testimony. When we recognize we are His – He uses us profoundly.

Author Tim Hansel tells the story about the day he and his son Zac were out in the country, climbing around in some cliffs. He heard a voice from above him yell, "Hey Dad! Catch me!" He turned around to see Zac joyfully jumping off a rock straight at him. Zac had first jumped and then yelled, "Hey Dad!" Tim became an instant circus act, catching Zac. They both fell to the ground. For a moment, after Tim caught Zac he could hardly talk. When he found his voice again, he gasped in exasperation: "Zac! Can you give me one good reason why you did that???" Zac responded with remarkable calmness: "Sure! Because you're my Dad." Zac's whole assurance was based on the fact that his father was trustworthy. He could live life to the hilt because his father could be trusted. **Don't forget! Dark Times are opportunities for light to make a real difference!**

Shine the Light
Lessons in Daniel

Lesson Four: Daniel 4:1-27 "Seven Steps to Effective Sharing of Truth"

You have an employee, and he keeps coming into work late. At first, it was a minute or two, and you overlooked it. In a matter of months, it increased, and almost every day he arrived ten to fifteen minutes after the appointed time and often left a few minutes early.

What should you do? You have essentially two choices available to convince them to do right:

- You can use what leadership experts call "SOFT persuasion," OR

- You can opt for "HARD persuasion."

Most of us are familiar with HARD persuasion from our homes. It sounds like this: "If you walk through that door one minute late again, you will be sent home without pay for the rest of the day!" Hard persuasion sounds to me like nice words for "threat." SOFT persuasion comes most often in the form of the "carrot" – not the "stick." In the case of soft persuasion, you might say to the employee something like this: "I know that you have been struggling to be on time, and I know I haven't said much in the past – but this is really getting to be a habit I cannot tolerate. Let's do this. If you will work at being on time every day for the next two months, I will reconsider that raise request you made last quarter. I am rooting for you to win, so that both of us will win!"

Let's be honest: some of us HATE the idea of the soft persuasion. We think the "carrot" approach is intrinsically weak and wimpy, and it grates us the wrong way. We were threatened when we were coming up through the ranks, and we want people to stop wimping out and suck it up and do their jobs – or get in the unemployment line. All this "whining" and "hand out" based culture has gotten under our skin.

Now, we walk into church, and you want to hear "straight truth" – you know, the kind that reminds us of Jonathan Edwards' *Sinners in the hands of an Angry God*. "C'mon preacher – give it to us! Don't soften sin – let 'em have it! Tell them that God is in Heaven about to **really unload** on this sin-sick nation of lazy and perverted men." Some believers seem to have been sucking green persimmons....

Let me ask you something. **Is fire and brimstone all that we have in the arsenal against a rising tide of ungodly promotions by people in power?** Can we offer both a positive word and a loving spirit amid darkening days of proud paganism and its arrogant boasting?

As we open the record of a believer of long ago, we will note that Daniel found significant ways to have a positive impact in very dark places without losing his grip on kindness and gentle force! God didn't just use him a long time ago, but provided the record that we might see and emulate him! This lesson isn't so much about <u>our message – which does not change – but about our method – which must adapt to the hearer.</u> Why? The answer is simple…

Key Principle: Effective outreach is when the world about us can truly hear what we are trying to say and respond correctly to it.

Before we delve into the writing of Daniel 4, it might be good to remind ourselves about the man whom God used to record the story. He was a believer, flawed but faithful. God superintended his writing to tell God's story. There are a few things to remember.

- Daniel offers a **theme** that demonstrates the absolute truth and superiority of "El Elyon" (the God of Abraham) over the entire world – Gentiles as well as Hebrews, as the Aramaic section of the book unfolds.

- **Daniel's life message was this: God is in charge of everyone – even those who don't believe in Him.**

- The book's theme appears to **shift** in emphasis when the Hebrew language resumes in chapter 8, focusing the control of God on the program He planned for His own people. God planned not only chastisement and shame for them (which they were experiencing surrounded by pagans) but a future restoration and prominence.

The point of the book seems to be this: **God is in charge.** He is in charge of those who GET that He is in charge – but He is also in charge of those who DON'T. He has a special and more complete message about events to those who BELIEVE, but He doesn't need man's belief to be fully SOVEREIGN.

The Situation in Chapter Four:

Let's move in on our story as we unfold the scroll to chapter four. We open the story in progress....Daniel was dropped on to a pagan campus, surrounded by godless men with their lusts for power and control – and God gave him opportunities to share the truth of His God unapologetically before them. A great example is unfolding. It began with a proclamation of a lesson learned by a great king of long ago. Listen to the proclamation and see if you can pick out the events that brought the story to this point:

Daniel 4:1 Nebuchadnezzar the king to all the peoples, nations, and [men of every] language that live in all the Earth: "May your peace abound! 2 It has seemed good to me to declare the signs and wonders which the Most High God has done for me. 3 How great are His signs and how mighty are His wonders! His kingdom is an everlasting kingdom and His dominion is from generation to generation. 4 I, Nebuchadnezzar, was at ease in my house and flourishing in my palace. 5 I saw a dream and it made me fearful; and [these] fantasies [as I lay] on my bed and the visions in my mind kept alarming me. 6 So I gave orders to bring into my presence all the wise men of Babylon that they might make known to me the interpretation of the dream. 7 Then the magicians, the conjurers, the Chaldeans and the diviners came in and I related the dream to them, but they could not make its interpretation known to me. 8 But finally Daniel came in before me, whose name is Belteshazzar according to the name of my god, and in whom is a spirit of the holy gods; and I related the dream to him, [saying], 9 'O Belteshazzar, chief of the magicians, since I know that a spirit of the holy gods is in you and no mystery baffles you, tell [me] the visions of my dream which I have seen, along with its interpretation.' 10 Now [these were] the visions in my mind [as I lay] on my bed: I was looking, and behold, [there was] a tree in the midst of the Earth and its height [was] great. 11 The tree grew large and became strong and its height reached to the sky, and it [was] visible to the end of the whole earth. 12 Its foliage [was] beautiful and its fruit abundant, and in it [was] food for all. The beasts of the field found shade under it, and the birds of the sky dwelt in its branches, and all living creatures fed themselves from it. 13 I was looking in the visions in my mind [as I lay] on my bed, and behold, an [angelic] watcher, a holy one, descended from Heaven. 14 He shouted out and spoke as follows: 'Chop down the tree and cut off its branches; strip off its foliage and scatter its fruit. Let the beasts flee from under it and the birds from its branches. 15 Yet leave the stump with its roots in the ground, but with a band of iron and bronze [around it] in the new grass of the field; and let him be drenched with the dew of Heaven, and let him share with the beasts in the grass of the earth. 16 Let his mind be changed from [that of] a man and let a beast's mind be given to him, and let seven periods of time pass over him.' 17 This sentence is by the decree of the [angelic] watchers and the decision is a command of the holy ones, in order that the living may know That the Most High is ruler over the realm of mankind, and bestows it on whom He wishes and sets over it the lowliest of men."

That's it. That was the opportunity that Daniel was given to look into the eyes of the most powerful man alive and tell him about the God of Heaven. Daniel stepped up to the task. Our lesson is about how he did it – because we are increasingly being called upon to share God's Word with people who have little connection to Him – and who know little of His love – like the king of long ago in this passage.

Notice **three things about the encounter** the king had, according to the official testimony:

- **First, he recognized in it that there were two worlds** – a physical one and a spiritual one. He showed some spiritual sensitivity to God. He wasn't just asking about theoretical ideology – he had an inkling that there was something spiritual happening.

- **Second, he wasn't prepared for the way the message intruded on his comfortable life.** God was at work – and it wasn't as a result of some search the king began.

- **Third, the king took from his encounter** (according to the decree) **a message** of God's Sovereignty and man as the subject of the Mighty One of Heaven. He got the point of the lesson after he encountered Daniel.

Lessons in Daniel: Shine the Light

Here is my question. **How did Daniel get the message across to the king?** Did he threaten him with hellfire and brimstone? Did he pander to him? How did he speak truth to power, but keep calm and not water down a tough message? It is a lesson for our time…

Seven Steps to Effective Sharing of Truth:

Daniel based his presentation on the REPUTATION of his life. (4:18)

Your life gives you the opportunity to speak into the lives of others.

Daniel 4:18 This is the dream [which] I, King Nebuchadnezzar, have seen. Now you, Belteshazzar, tell [me] its interpretation, inasmuch as none of the wise men of my kingdom is able to make known to me the interpretation; but you are able, for a spirit of the holy gods is in you.

Build your testimony in every life choice you make – big and small. People follow YOU before they follow your message. Live the clarity of your message.

Jesus can be seen BEST in a life that doesn't cloud His reflection. Maybe it is best to offer a simple illustration:

A reporter once asked Albert Einstein's wife if she understood the theory of relativity. She replied, "No, but I know Albert, and he can be trusted."

Don't forget that people are ALWAYS watching your life. There are times when I have – and I have always regretted it. I think of an old story that helps me remember that people have their eye on my choices:

A bus driver gave the new visiting preacher too much change. The pastor sat in his seat, looked at the change, and was conflicted. He was new to town and didn't want to make a big deal, but he was sure he got too much change. After a few minutes on the ride, the pastor went to the driver and said, "Excuse me sir, I am new in town, so I may not have figured this whole thing out, but it looks to me like I got too much money back in change." The driver replied, "Many thanks! I knew that you were the new pastor in town and I just wanted to decide whether I wanted to go to your church or not!" (A-Z Sermon Illustrations)

Notice that Daniel wasn't trying to show with his life that HE was more capable – but the passage clearly stated that the king knew it was the INDWELLING of God's Spirit that made him able.

It isn't our job to make people think we are great – because we aren't. It is our job to allow the work of God within us to shine through our lives and touch them. In the time of trouble, they will acknowledge that God has been working there, and they noticed it before.

Daniel showed SINCERE CARING for Nebuchadnezzar. (4:19) Even when he shared hard words, he did it with a heart broken to have harm come to the king.

Daniel 4:19 Then Daniel, whose name is Belteshazzar, was appalled for a while as his thoughts alarmed him. The king responded and said, "Belteshazzar, do not let the dream or its interpretation alarm you." Belteshazzar replied, "My lord, [if only] the dream applied to those who hate you and its interpretation to your adversaries!"
Wasn't this the king that took him from his home country in 606 BCE? Why should he care?

You will not have a positive impact on people that believe that you hate them – even if you totally disagree with their life choices. It is in both loving them and in speaking truth that we reach effectively into the lives of others.

In an article in *Campus Life* a young nurse writes of her pilgrimage in learning to see in a patient the image of God beneath a very "distressing disguise." Eileen was one of her first patients, a person who was totally helpless. "A cerebral aneurysm (broken blood vessels in the brain) had left her with no conscious control over her body," the nurse wrote. "As near as the doctors could tell Eileen was totally unconscious, unable to feel pain and unaware of anything going on around her. It was the job of the hospital staff to turn her every hour to prevent bedsores and to feed her twice a day, 'what looked like a thin mush through a stomach tube.'" Caring for her was a thankless task. "When it's this bad," an older student nurse told her, "you have to detach yourself emotionally from the whole situation…" As a result, more and more Eileen came to be treated as a thing, a vegetable … But the young student nurse decided that she could not treat Eileen as the others had treated her. She talked to her, sang to her, encouraged her and even brought her little gifts. One day when things were especially difficult and it would have been easy for the young nurse to take out her frustrations on the patient, she was especially kind. It was Thanksgiving Day and the nurse said to the patient, "I was in a cruddy mood this morning, Eileen, because it was supposed to be my day off. But now that I'm here, I'm glad. I wouldn't have wanted to miss seeing you on Thanksgiving. Do you know this is Thanksgiving?" Just then, the telephone rang, and as the nurse turned to answer it, she looked quickly back at the patient. "Suddenly," she writes, "Eileen was looking at me … crying. Big damp circles stained her pillow, and she was shaking all over." That was the only human emotion that Eileen ever showed any of them, but it was enough to change the whole attitude of the hospital staff toward her. Not long afterward, Eileen died. The young nurse closes her story, saying, "I keep thinking about her … It occurred to me that I owe her an awful lot. Except for Eileen, I might never have known what it's like to give myself to someone who can't give back."

Men and women, we must stop seeing people in the abstract – and see them as God's wondrous creations! The most heinous example of a loose-living celebrity, caustic to our faith with their every sentence, must be seen differently than our fallen heart desires to consider. Disdain is not the beginning of outreach, love is. In an effort to be clear about right and wrong in a day when that clarity has been lost in the public square, many of us have turned sour and mean. We have to admit it, because soured hearts are not surrendered ones….

Can we not see that the absolute worst nightmare of a politician in our day is STILL a man or woman – a person with feelings, hopes aspirations and dreams? They get cold in the blowing wind, and they have times of loneliness and boredom. They aren't JUST the public persona of the media – they are people. We must remember to see them as God's created beings or we will speak of them as things – and that won't reach anyone. Jesus made them. He loved them enough to come and die for them. We must recall the caring in our hearts and voices to reach lost people.

Daniel wasn't short on PRAISE FOR GOOD THINGS in the life of the one that was not living what God desired. (4:20-22).

He wasn't faking it, or "apple polishing" – that wasn't his style. He was praising what he could! (4:20-22)

Daniel 4:20 The tree that you saw, which became large and grew strong, whose height reached to the sky and was visible to all the Earth 21 and whose foliage [was] beautiful and its fruit abundant, and in which [was] food for all, under which the beasts of the field dwelt and in whose branches the birds of the sky lodged—22 it is you, O king; for you have become great and grown strong, and your majesty has become great and reached to the sky and your dominion to the end of the Earth.

We have to be observant for good things, and we have to admit we don't always know the value of things, much less of people!
We hear stories like that of Ted and Virginia from Arizona. Their story was found on "Antiques Roadshow" a few years back on PBS. Ted inherited a blanket from an aunt, and not caring much for the blanket, just threw it on a chair in the bedroom. There it stayed for years until the "Antiques Roadshow" came through Tucson. Just for kicks, Ted and Virginia carried the blanket (the aunt told them it was Kit Carson's) to see if it was worth anything, thinking perhaps it might be worth a couple of thousand dollars. Donald Ellis was the appraiser that day, and he almost fainted when he saw the blanket. Turns out the blanket was an original Navajo creation dating to the early 1800's, of which only fifty remain in existence, and none in the condition of Ted and Virginia's. Mr. Ellis appraised the blanket on the show for $350,000. Ted and Virginia sold the blanket at auction for close to half a million dollars. From trash to treasure indeed! (Author unknown)

Can we not readily admit that we are adept at picking out the flaws of people, but are far less able to quickly cite what is GOOD about them? If you want to reach people, you must become a student of people – able to see more keenly their possibilities and not simply their flaws.

Daniel SPOKE TRUTH but with a broken heart for his king! (4:23)

I think it is important that we recognize that he didn't shrink back and compromise the truth, but he also didn't enjoy the message of judgment.

Daniel 4:23 In that the king saw an [angelic] watcher, a holy one, descending from Heaven and saying, "Chop down the tree and destroy it; yet leave the stump with its roots in the ground, but with a band of iron and bronze [around it] in the new grass of the field, and let him be drenched with the dew of Heaven, and let him share with the beasts of the field until seven periods of time pass over him,"

A teenage boy was diagnosed with cancer and as a result was in the hospital for several weeks to undergo radiation treatments and chemotherapy. During that time, he lost all of his hair. On the way home from the hospital, he was worried - not about the cancer, but about the embarrassment & shame of going back to school with a baldhead. He was afraid of being laughed at, ridiculed, & mocked. He had already decided not to wear a wig or a hat. When he arrived home, he walked in the front door and turned on the lights. To his surprise, about fifty of his friends jumped up and shouted, "Welcome home!"' The boy looked around the room and could hardly believe his eyes - all fifty of his friends had shaved their heads! Wouldn't we all like to have caring friends who were so sensitive and committed to us that they would sacrifice their hair for us if that's what it took to make us feel affirmed, included, and loved? (Sermon central illustrations)

The friends didn't change the truth of the situation, but they communicated a heart to walk through the fire with their friend!
Daniel didn't flinch in the message to try to change the coming judgment of the king – he delivered the message faithfully, though he knew the horror of its sound. Consider this: the message that the king was soon to be reduced to an animal needed to be delivered to the king to whom the message was aimed. **It wasn't Daniel's choice to make it happen, but it was his job to deliver the message no matter how he felt about it.**

Let me ask you to do something: Make sure you feel the pain of hell for those in our world before you proclaim it as the destination of lost men. I don't want to flinch, but I want to feel the message. Cold hearts reach no one, and spread only death. Feel pain when the Gospel makes clear the requirement to know Christ for life eternal – or something is missing inside you that God wants to use.

Daniel CONNECTED THE MESSAGE to God's perspective on the future judgment. (4:24-25)

Not a single sentence of interpretation was offered by Daniel that wasn't smothered with the sauce of God's decree. Daniel wasn't offering HIS idea, but telling God's path forward…

Daniel 4:24 This is the interpretation, O king, and this is the decree of the Most High, which has come upon my lord the king: 25 that you be driven away from mankind and your dwelling place be with the beasts of the field, and you be given grass to eat like cattle and be drenched with the dew of heaven; and seven periods of time will pass over you, until you recognize that the Most High is ruler over the realm of mankind and bestows it on whomever He wishes.

We have the privilege of connecting God's Word to people's lives in a positive way.

This characteristic was well demonstrated by the nineteenth century missionary named John Selwyn, sent to the South Pacific, after having built a reputation as a renowned boxer and man of great strength. During his years in the South Pacific, he had occasion to strongly rebuke a native, and that native struck him violently across his face. Selwyn responded by folding his arms and looking intently into the eyes of the native, who realized that Selwyn could easily have knocked him cold. But Selwyn made not the slightest effort to retaliate and simply gazed at him with loving concern. The native ran into the jungle, too ashamed to face this missionary. Several years after John Selwyn had returned home, that same native came forward to confess Christ and be baptized by Selwyn's replacement. When asked what new name he wished to be called by, the native replied, "Call me John Selwyn, for it was he who taught me what Jesus Christ is like." (Sermon central illustrations)

Daniel looked the king in the eye and said, "You are going to eat grass and lie in the field." Yet, he didn't stop there. <u>He connected the truth to the lesson:</u> **God is going to teach you something you need to know through the experience.** He didn't have an enviable position, but he had a necessary one – and so do we.

Daniel SHOWED THE HOPE of the return of the king! (4:26)

The message of God offered hope even in the face of judgment – that is why God offered it! He kept speaking…

Daniel 4:26 And in that it was commanded to leave the stump with the roots of the tree, your kingdom will be assured to you after you recognize that [it is] Heaven [that] rules.

In the *Bible*, God offered a message of judgment to a man facing judgment… and you need to ask a simple question. Why would He do that? Why not just take the man off the throne and put him out to pasture? Why not simply conclude that the man refused to follow God and His Word, and so he should be left to his own judgment?

Men and women, we don't understand God at all when we conclude such things. That fact, that the king was a sinner who did not yield to God, has been true of every member of our race since Adam's sin in the Garden of Eden. There have been no natural exceptions – though there was one unnaturally introduced Messiah to that scene. The message of hope is the message of the Cross. God JUDGED your sin in Christ – and wants your life surrendered. The HOPE of the message is found in this truth: we don't have to face the end without the knowledge of what God is saying… and even more….

Daniel OFFERED AN ALTERNATIVE to the coming judgment. (4:27)

We don't have to face the end without the opportunity to avert the coming judgment altogether. It is our simple choice…

Daniel 4:27 Therefore, O king, may my advice be pleasing to you: break away now from your sins by [doing] righteousness and from your iniquities by showing mercy to [the] poor, in case there may be a prolonging of your prosperity.'

Many of us act in our lives as if we are forced to continue in rebellion against God. Yielding may be TOUGH, but it is not IMPOSSIBLE!

I think of something author Gary Thomas wrote years ago about people in marriage disputes….He wrote: "I don't believe couples fall out of love—they fall out of repentance." (*Putting Yourself Last, Marriage Partnership,* Winter 1999)

Can you see it? You aren't forced to follow a wrong direction – we are CHOOSING to face judgment by not accepting God's way out… That is our message. That is how we can be heard…

Effective outreach is when they can hear what we truly are trying to say and respond to it.

Let me close with a simple story that says what Daniel was doing in one single paragraph, and ask the believers pulling through this lesson to consider "getting on board." Author and teacher, Dr. Howard Hendricks tells the story of a young man who strayed from the Lord but was finally brought back by the help of a friend who really loved him. When there was full repentance and restoration, Dr. Hendricks asked this Christian how it felt away from the Lord. The young man said it seemed like he was out at sea, in deep water, deep trouble, and all his friends were on the shore hurling biblical accusations at him about justice, penalty, and wrong. "But, there was one Christian brother who actually swam out to get me and would not let me go. I fought him, but he pushed aside my fighting, grasped me, put a life jacket around me, and took me to shore. By the grace of God, he was the reason I was restored. He would not let me go." (Sermon central illustrations)

Why not consider dropping the rock of accusation on the shore, and taking a swim out to a struggling friend?

Shine the Light
Lessons in Daniel

Lesson Five: Daniel 5:1-31 "Rescue from the Forgotten"

When Paul McCartney was sixteen years old, his father turned sixty-four. That birthday inspired one of the first songs the young would-be "Beatle" ever wrote. The song was an imaginary conversation between a young man to his young love interest about "growing old together." Some of us smile at the young man's notion that "sixty-four" was so very old, especially in light of the fact that McCartney is seventy-two this year (born in 1942).

The song was on the Beatles playlist in the early days of their live concert circuit as an emergency "back-up" song to perform if their amplifiers blew a tube or power was disrupted. McCartney, with the wit and wisdom of his sixteen years of life wrote these words:

> I could be handy mending a fuse, when your lights have gone. You can knit a sweater by the fireside, Sunday mornings go for a ride. Doing the garden, digging the weeds, who could ask for more? Will you still need me? Will you still feed me, when I'm sixty-four?

That little window into English cottage living in the sixties is telling. McCartney clearly didn't know that sixty-four would one day be a great age for "skydiving" and "para-sailing in the Caribbean." I love it when the wisdom of youth is challenged by the innovation and energy of adulthood.

I don't know how I will feel at sixty-four, but I am not thinking Dottie will be sitting and knitting by the fireside, hoping I will take her out for a ride, unless we have flying cars by then. What I DO know, is that life isn't over at sixty-four, or (for that matter) at eighty-four. We don't come with "toe tags" and "expiration dates." We live until God says we are done living. As for me, I want to champion living until I don't. I don't want to EXIST; I want to LIVE!

One of my heroes in the *Bible* is the prophetic writer and former Prime Minister named Daniel. He lived, worked, and ministered well into his eighties. In our lesson from Daniel 5, we read of a time when he was quite old, taken out of sequence because his memoirs are written thematically. He was in his eighties – and that was as old as dirt a world with an average life expectancy that didn't break the mid-fifties. He was ANCIENT and though respected, not considered part of the "life blood" of his day on the political talk shows. He was the guy you interviewed in retrospectives, or when the guest of the day suddenly cancelled due to an impending crisis. Daniel was OLD NEWS, but God had a plan to dust him off and blow the pungent smell of mothballs – and put him back in the center of the story yet again.

Key Principle: To offer a positive message, we must stay engaged in the world that needs truth while longing for the life to come! We are never "off the hook" of ministry until we are with the Lord.

We all laugh at aging, because we all face it. For the young, just appropriately roll your eyes for a moment as we, who have greying hair, poke a bit of fun at ourselves…You have read these shared widely on the internet…I am sure…they are called: "You Know You're Getting Old When":

- Your joints are more accurate than the National Weather Service.

- Your investment in health insurance is finally beginning to pay off.
- Your back goes out more often than you do.
- The twinkle in your eye is only the reflection of the sun on your bifocals.
- You wake up with that morning-after feeling and you didn't do anything the night before.
- You don't care where your wife goes, just so you don't have to go along.
- Many of your co-workers were born the same year that you got your last promotion.
- People call at 9 PM and ask, "Did I wake you?"
- The pharmacist has become your new best friend.
- There's nothing left to learn the hard way.
- You come to the conclusion that your worst enemy is gravity.
- Your idea of a night out is sitting on the patio.
- You wake up, looking like your driver's license picture.
- Happy hour is a nap.
- You begin every other sentence with, "Nowadays…"
- You constantly talk about the price of gasoline.
- You don't remember when your wild oats turned to shredded wheat.
- You sing along with the elevator music.
- You are proud of your lawn mower.
- You wonder how you could be over the hill when you don't remember being on top of it.
- The little gray-haired lady you help across the street is your wife.
- Your secrets are safe with your friends because they can't remember them either.
- Your ears are hairier than your head.
- It takes longer to rest than it did to get tired.
- Your childhood toys are now in a museum.
- You confuse having a clear conscience with having a bad memory.
- You know all the answers, but nobody asks you the questions.
- You enjoy hearing about other people's operations.
- Your new easy chair has more options than your car.

- Your little black book only contains names ending in M.D.
- You get into a heated argument about pension plans. (original source unknown).

With our smiles and laughter, here is a SERIOUS QUESTION: Do you ever feel too old to be relevant?

Look for a few minutes at the story of a man who got older, but didn't become so stiff in nature that God could not and would not entrust new ministry to him in the lives of other people. His story shows that a man of integrity can live according to the beliefs he obtained by God's touch in his youth.

How did he stay pliable and useful to God? I believe if you examine the story recorded in this chapter, you will see at least **four practical ways he "stayed handy" for the work of God** to his generation.

Before we explore the four ways Daniel stayed "in the game" of life, let's make sure we recognize some truths about the passage the lesson is taken from.

First, the story is out of sequence in the book, and Daniel was much younger in the last lesson (and will be younger again later in the book). This is a selection from his life that God placed into the narrative to say something important.

The WORLD may say the young are at the center of everything, but God does not. He uses the young, with their vitality and hope, their zeal and their energy. Yet, He uses also the aging, with life experience and tempering in the world. God wants to use BOTH, and use them in harmony with one another!

Consider for a few moments the fact that Daniel reckoned ENGAGEMENT would keep him useful to God... There were

FIVE REASONS Daniel stayed engaged...and resisted the temptation to retreat and disconnect:

He stayed engaged in lives, because his world placed great weight on a false foundation!

He recognized he lived in a restless age with a pagan core. (5:1-4) Drop into the scene and see if you can pick out what he observed:

Daniel 5:1 Belshazzar the king held a great feast for a thousand of his nobles, and he was drinking wine in the presence of the thousand. 2 When Belshazzar tasted the wine, he gave orders to bring the gold and silver vessels which Nebuchadnezzar his father had taken out of the temple which was in Jerusalem, so that the king and his nobles, his wives and his concubines might drink from them. 3 Then they brought the gold vessels that had been taken out of the temple, the house of God which was in Jerusalem; and the king and his nobles, his wives and his concubines drank from them. 4 They drank the wine and praised the gods of gold and silver, of bronze, iron, wood and stone.

Let me set the scene a bit.

The year was 538 BCE. King Nabonidas, co-ruler of the Babylon Empire, was in a large plain outside the city with his army defending it against the mighty army of the Medes and Persians under Cyrus – a renegade ruler of the nearby emerging empire of the Medes and Persians. Babylon was considered impregnable, and the older Babylonian army had a world reputation for victory. The Persians were upstarts, a newly banded army that was threatening a super power of its day.

According to Herodotus, the historian's still disputed measures, the city had a wall surrounding it nearly 300 feet high and eighty feet wide, surrounded by deep moats. Any attempt to breach that wall must have seemed pointless – and that is what made the exercise of defense one of such confidence that inside the city a party could be held in a time of conflict. The archaeological data suggests the moat extended 35 feet into the ground. If one were to ride around the city outside the wall, he would travel 60 miles – it was a HUGE city by ancient standards. (Consider the trip Nehemiah made around Jerusalem a few years later that took a few hours through rubble). The wall of Babylon reportedly had some two hundred fifty guard towers and rooms for soldiers to sleep. It had upwards of one hundred gates, all armored with brass. If an enemy soldier managed to climb over the wall, he would have to cross a quarter mile of bare land before he could reach the city.

In addition, there was enough food warehoused for a twenty year siege and farmland within the wall to raise more if needed. The Euphrates River flowed under the wall to provide water for the crops, and had a cage fence to guard access by the river. While Nabonidas was defending the city against its enemies, his regent son, Belshazzar was inside the palace feasting with all the kingdom's nobles. Neither of them knew it was the last day of the mighty Babylonian empire…

Nabonidus (556-539 BCE) was a skilled general and field tactician; but a poor politician. He rebuilt temples of older gods, and tried to revive older moral tenets, but largely failed because he offended contemporary priests and lost popular support of the young, who were looking for something new and "hip." His son and regent was Belshazzar, the holder of the crown for his father during his many military exploits (ruled 549 until the 539 takeover by Persian Cyrus II) and administrator of the empire while his father stayed at Teima in western Arabia in the latter years.

Don't miss the background – **OLD SCHOOL KING** and **youthful and boisterous generation**… and Daniel lived in the city, probably in a school teaching, or studying old scrolls and keeping watch on the city with other shuffleboard-playing scholars… Yet, he didn't lose touch with the observations of the false foundation. There are **ways he could see it:**

Daniel recognized the generation had "false beliefs" they held dear. The very name of the prince betrayed his paganism.

5:1a Belshazzar: "Bel protect the king!"

The prince followed a religion and based his life on a god of his own making – not a god that required anything of him! One of the valuable lessons those who have been on the planet for longer will be able to readily observe is this: **People often live life as though they get to determine what truth is; and what eternity and the god that judges them is like!** That presumes that there is NO Creator.

If there is ONE GOD, then your beliefs about Him must square with the truth of Who He is – or your service to Him will be in error. If He cares about such things, your life and future will be in peril. People who make up their own rules do so because they do not accept the notion that TRUTH exists outside of them – and they must find and follow it – not invent it.

Daniel recognized that people were living in "false security."

5:1b: ...held a great feast...

Archaeologists have unearthed a banquet room that would seat ten thousand people – an astounding sized party in a time when capital cities of some kingdoms could not hold that number! Daniel recognized the threats of the times were significant, even if the partiers carried on like stocks were secure, and their dollar was unassailable. The prince's father was fighting a losing battle without, but Belshazzar seemed utterly disconnected from peril – you know the type. People seem to disconnect from the problems of life around them and live as though the issues will not affect them – unfortunately, they will!

Daniel recognized that people mistook excess for happiness, but it was a sham.

5:1b-2 ...drinking wine in the presence of the thousand.

Belshazzar the prince exemplified the playboy philosophy so prevalent in a paganized society. The end and goal of life seems to be to provide constant satisfaction and ongoing pleasure for the body. The terms used in the text are unmistakable – Belshazzar was at least impaired and at most drunk. He was using the resources of the kingdom to satiate his desires, not to maintain order and prepare for war.

Even when the threat is clearly at the door, many people tend to try to find an escape from impending crises and hope they will be averted – unfortunately, they seldom are!

Daniel could see through the false value system boasted superiority over God and His worship.

5:2b-3 ...bring the gold and silver vessels...taken out of the temple which was in Jerusalem.

The hedonistic philosophy is: "If you want it, get it. If it feels good, do it." You don't have to be fabulously wealthy to have this attitude, either. Many in our society live this way on nothing but credit. **This philosophy has no place for a God Who places demands and expects moral purity from His followers.** Pagans exhibit the reality that nothing is sacred to them. These vessels were carefully inventoried (see Ezra and the numbers of them) and were kept by his ancestors in respect to the gods they conquered. He sat on the throne, but had none of the respectful values of those before him. He was going to give the vessels for common use among the dignitaries ("noble") but also to the concubines (ignoble uses). Sensual living tends to stupefy! People often scorn the values of the past and the respect system believing we don't need the old conventions – unfortunately, they will discover they are wrong!

The king and his men forgot what (or better WHO) provided the great wealth of their land! How like them we can be!

Some years ago, a young man approached the foreman of a logging crew and asked for a job. "That depends," replied the foreman. "Let's see you fell this tree." The young man stepped forward and skillfully felled a great tree. Impressed, the foreman exclaimed, "Start Monday!" Monday, Tuesday, Wednesday, Thursday rolled by, and Thursday afternoon the foreman approached the young man and said, "You can pick up your paycheck on the way out today." Startled, he replied, "I thought you paid on Friday." "Normally we do," answered the foreman, "but we're letting you go today because you've fallen behind. Our daily felling charts show that you've dropped from first place on Monday to last on Wednesday." "But I'm a hard worker," the young man objected. "I arrive first, leave last, and even have worked through my coffee breaks!" The foreman, sensing the boy's integrity thought for a minute and then asked, "Have you been sharpening your ax?" The young man replied, "I've been working too hard to take the time." Remember how we got where we are! (Author unknown)

In our day, the message could not be clearer:

- When you dismiss the Creator, you begin to erode the inalienable rights our fathers fought to preserve. If there is no God above them, there will be no reason to expect men of means will care deeply for those with nothing.

- When you crush the family, you forget the first place people were instructed to find the meanings of words like "responsibility, loyalty and fidelity." The home will be reflected in the public square quickly.

- When you demean human life by killing the inconvenient, you diminish the whole basic value of society. When the value of life is dismissed, and the value of liberty is curtailed – only the value of the pursuit of happiness is left.

Daniel recognized the people became belligerent against truth.

5:4 ...they praised the gods of gold and silver.

The prince was totally insensitive to the demands of God and the feelings of God's people. He became sensual, materialistic, and blasphemous. Belshazzar didn't hesitate to openly blaspheme the God Who held Belshazzar's life and future in His hands. The people decided the work of their hands was the measure of success – and that ended them.

They blocked the thoughts of eternity, even though the *Bible* says in *Ecclesiastes 3:11 (New International Version) He has made everything beautiful in its time. He has also set eternity in the hearts of men; yet they cannot fathom what God has done from beginning to end.*

They set aside eternity and measured life by the NOW. People measure life by what they have attained and gained and not what they have become. People who are taught to emphasize rights and live for physical pleasures make poor society builders...

Daniel stayed in touch with society. He didn't buy into it, but he didn't sit and bark at it either. He was useful to God because he wasn't out of touch with the world around him, but kept himself actively observing the problems, and evaluating the issues. Maybe many days no one listened to what he had to say – but when they did – he HAD something to say. It wasn't simply about what he learned years before, but about what was happening at that time. Daniel was ENGAGED in the world around him because he wanted to be ready for God to use his life – and HE KNEW THE WORLD AROUND HIM WAS LIVING BASED ON THE WRONG PREMISE.

Daniel stayed engaged because God hasn't finished His work yet! (5:5-6)

Daniel 5:5 Suddenly, the fingers of a man's hand emerged and began writing opposite the lampstand on the plaster of the wall of the king's palace, and the king saw the back of the hand that did the writing. 6 Then the king's face grew pale and his thoughts alarmed him, and his hip joints went slack and his knees began knocking together.

Don't forget that God will move according to His own timing, and we must be there to assist the people faced with God's revelation.

5:5a Suddenly...

God offered no more warning than the revelation of the Word of God itself. Remember Luke 16 and the rich man – send them one from the dead that they may avoid the troubles was answered with – "They have the Law and the Prophets!" Don't think that troubles will come with skywriting – we have 1189 chapters of truth that are already ignored by most people... The problem isn't that God hasn't spoken, warned, explained and exposed the plan...

It is also worth noting that people who know God reverence Him and invite Him into their lives; people who don't will FEAR Him when they meet Him!

5:5b-6 ...the fingers of a man's hand...

The term "handwriting on the wall" has become synonymous with judgment. When it came, Belshazzar knew it was a power beyond his, but there was little he could do to stop it or change the words written. He was so frightened his face turned pale and his knees knocked together. If you challenge God to a duel, you'd better have a pistol that can fire a billion miles a millisecond – or you will find yourself completely mismatched.

Daniel stayed engaged because he knew God wasn't done writing His story. The world wasn't over – and neither was HE. <u>As long as we have breath, we have a ministry.</u>

Daniel stayed engaged because people around him were blind without a representative of God's people – and he didn't leave his post expecting someone else to pick it up until he was gone. (5:7-12)

Daniel 5:7 The king called aloud to bring in the conjurers, the Chaldeans and the diviners. The king spoke and said to the wise men of Babylon, "Any man who can read this inscription and explain its interpretation to me shall be clothed with purple and have a necklace of gold around his neck, and have authority as third ruler in the kingdom." 8 Then all the king's wise men came in, but they could not read the inscription or make known its interpretation to the king. 9 Then King Belshazzar was greatly alarmed, his face grew even paler, and his nobles were perplexed. 10 The queen entered the banquet hall because of the words of the king and his nobles; the queen spoke and said, "O king, live forever! Do not let your thoughts alarm you or your face be pale. 11 There is a man in your kingdom in whom is a spirit of the holy gods; and in the days of your father, illumination, insight and wisdom like the wisdom of the gods were found in him. And King Nebuchadnezzar, your father, your father the king, appointed him chief of the magicians, conjurers, Chaldeans and diviners. 12 This was because an extraordinary spirit, knowledge and insight, interpretation of dreams, explanation of enigmas and solving of difficult problems were found in this Daniel, whom the king named Belteshazzar. Let Daniel now be summoned and he will declare the interpretation."

I cannot help but feel that people without a walk with God and a knowledge of His Word are like blind leading the blind. Look at the phrase: "...the king called." People will look for answers among people who have no more clue than they do! The men couldn't explain the truth, because they couldn't see the truth! Without an ability to pull off a good life, we pay men and women literally hundreds of thousands to educate the upcoming generation. What would happen if we actually demanded a "track record" of example from them BEFORE they became teachers of our young? What if a professor had to actually show him or herself to be a good person in order to be qualified to help shape lives of our youth? Daniel didn't complain; he stayed a part of the conversation of his community. People TRUSTED him, and that became his platform to speak. Youth haven't had time to build that platform, and Daniel didn't trade it away – but kept it for use until his last breath.

Daniel recognized that he was God's representative: "There is a man..." Look at the description:

- **Testimony:** *In whom is the spirit* – the recognition was about THEN, not just about the past. **Can people STILL see God active in your life?**

- **Consistency:** *In the days of your father...* Look at the reality that the testimony of former years wasn't being replaced by FOLLY in later years. **Can people count on continued maturity and wisdom from you?**

To offer a positive message, we must stay engaged in the world that needs truth while longing for the life to come! We cannot retire from truth and we dare not leave our post until God calls us home. We must stay actively engaged in our walk with

God, and continue to add to the old testimony NEW ENCOUNTERS with God and other people!

Daniel stayed engaged, because he had lived long enough not be bought off by trinkets that meant little in the longer frame of life. (5:13-17)

Daniel 5: 13 Then Daniel was brought in before the king. The king spoke and said to Daniel, "Are you that Daniel who is one of the exiles from Judah, whom my father the king brought from Judah? ...15 Just now the wise men and the conjurers were brought in before me that they might read this inscription and make its interpretation known to me, but they could not declare the interpretation of the message. 16 But I personally have heard about you, that you are able to give interpretations and solve difficult problems... 17 Then Daniel answered and said before the king, "Keep your gifts for yourself or give your rewards to someone else; however, I will read the inscription to the king and make the interpretation known to him."

By the time Daniel was called in before the king, fortune he couldn't use meant little. Fame was only a bother to him when he took walks in the city. Power was something he had much of in his life, and watched it pay few lasting dividends. Pleasure was limited to a good stew, a warm fire and some pleasant company.

What I am trying to say is that he had grown in life to see the world for what it was – a temporary mess that held fleeting joys. Life is GOOD, but it isn't the final object for the person who understands the value of knowing God and living for the eternal. That is your strength as a believer. You can enjoy good food, but not get lost in the need for bigger and more elaborate banquets. You can laugh without needing endless folly. You can see the difference between people who are using people to get "ahead" and people who know that the front of the line isn't much better than the back of it. Daniel stayed engaged because he could add a sense of reality to a world lost in the search for filling pockets with holes and insatiable appetites.

Daniel stayed engaged so that when his moment came, he was ready to be used of God! (5:13-29)

The story concluded:

Daniel 5:18 "O king, the Most High God granted sovereignty, grandeur, glory and majesty to Nebuchadnezzar your father... 22 Yet you, his son, Belshazzar, have not humbled your heart, even though you knew all this, 23 but you have exalted yourself against the Lord of Heaven; and they have brought the vessels of His house before you, and you and your nobles; your wives and your concubines have been drinking wine from them; and you have praised the gods of silver and gold, of bronze, iron, wood and stone, which do not see, hear or understand. But the God in whose hand are your life-breath and all your ways, you have not glorified. 24 Then the hand was sent from Him and this inscription was written out. 25 Now this is the inscription that was written out, 'MENE, MENE, TEKEL, UPHARSIN.' 26 This is the interpretation of the message: 'MENE'—God has numbered your kingdom and put an end to it. 27 'TEKEL'—you have been weighed on the scales and found deficient. 28 'PERES'—your kingdom has been divided and given over to the Medes and Persians." 29 Then Belshazzar gave orders, and they clothed Daniel with purple and put a necklace of gold around his neck, and issued a proclamation concerning him that he now had authority as the third ruler in the kingdom.

God provided a testimony by means of His engaged servant. This was a man who lived his disciplines daily. Let me warn you – disengagement is an undisciplined life! The enemy of staying engaged is the "but first" syndrome – that robs our days of accomplishment... Someone explained it this way:

I have recently been diagnosed with the "But First Syndrome." You know, it's when I decide to do the laundry. I start down the hall and notice the newspaper on the table. OK, I'm going to do the laundry...BUT FIRST, I'm going to read the newspaper. Then, I notice the mail on the table. OK, I'll just put the newspaper in the recycle stack....

- BUT FIRST, I'll look through that pile of mail and see if there are any bills to be paid. Yes, now where's the checkbook? Oop's... There's the empty glass from yesterday on the coffee table. I'm going to look for that checkbook....

- BUT FIRST, I need to put the glass in the sink. I head for the kitchen, look out the window, and notice my poor flowers need a drink of water. I put the glass in the sink, and darn it, there's the remote for the TV on the kitchen counter. What's it doing here? I'll just put it away....

- BUT FIRST, I need to water those plants... Head for the door and... Aaaagh! Stepped on the cat. Cat needs to be fed. Okay, I'll put that remote away and water the plants...

- BUT FIRST, I need to feed the cat...

By the end of day: laundry is not done, newspapers are still on the floor, glass is still in the sink, bills are unpaid, checkbook is still lost, and the cat ate the remote control... And, when I try to figure out how come nothing got done all day, I'm baffled because... (Author unknown). I want to call you to remain engaged. Don't substitute RAGE with ENGAGEMENT! Don't grouse instead of praying. Be stirred, but not soured by life. God has you here for a purpose! **To offer a positive message, we must stay engaged in the world that needs truth while longing for the life to come!**

Shine the Light
Lessons in Daniel

Lesson Six: Daniel 6:1-28 "Five Critical Choices"

Have you ever encountered a worker that goes "above and beyond" to help you? I have had the privilege of meeting quite a number of them as I travel and speak, and enjoy a rich life in my work experiences. I have concluded from God's Word something I want to share with you: If you know the Lord, and as a result, you decide to be an honest, faithful, diligent employee, God will honor and bless you – perhaps in this life but surely the next.

I want to tell you a true story that I think may encourage you…
A number of years ago, an elderly man and his wife arrived by train in the city of Chicago. It was a stormy night and their train had been delayed. It was after midnight when they finally arrived at a downtown hotel they hoped had a vacancy. The young clerk on duty that night was named George Boldt and he explained that because there were three different conventions in town, their hotel was full, but he would be glad to call around and check with some other hotels. After several calls, it was clear that there were no empty rooms to be found. The young clerk said to the couple, "I can't send a nice couple like you out into the rain on a night like this. Would you be willing to sleep in my room in the basement? It's not large, but it's clean and I don't need it tonight because I'm on duty." The couple gladly accepted his offer. The next morning the man tried to pay George personally, but the young clerk refused. Then the man said to George Boldt, "You're the kind of man who ought to be the boss of the best hotel in America. Maybe one day I'll build one for you." The young clerk only smiled and said, "I was just glad to be of service." Several years later George Boldt received a letter with train ticket to New York City. The old gentleman took him to

the corner of 5th Avenue and 54th Street in Manhattan and said, "This is the hotel I have built for you to manage." George Boldt stared in awe and said, "Are you joking?" It was no joke. The old man's name was William Waldorf Astor. And that's how George Boldt became the first manager of the Waldorf Astoria Hotel. If you go to New York City, there is George's portrait hanging in the lobby, a tribute to a clerk who showed integrity and went the second mile.

Most of us know people who 'go the extra mile' in the job – and they are encouraging to us. In days when it seems like so many people show up on the job and consider us – the client – a MAJOR INCONVENIENCE to their day, the 'extra mile' worker is a refreshing change. Now since this isn't a business seminar or a motivational speech about working hard – you may wonder WHY I began with this story. In the familiar pages of God's Word, there is a story about God's blessing to an obedient and positive hearted servant. The well-known story of "Daniel in the lion's den" illustrates dramatically the idea that a positive view of life is about choices, not simply about life circumstances. Daniel knew that life dedicated and surrendered to God would not be EASY, but it would be a POSITIVE experience if he kept his commitment to God at the center of his life, and evaluated his experiences as something prescribed by his God.

Key Principle: Your ability to be positive has more to do with your life choices than your life circumstances!

Here is the truth: Life can be hard, but God is not hard-hearted. He loves you, and He knows you. If you know Him, and if you have made the choice to follow Him through the conditions carefully prescribed in His Word, you will find that a positive life is about living out that choice properly.

Let's look at this familiar story, and see if we can pick out the **choices** Daniel **made to be POSITIVE about life,** despite challenges deliberately placed in his path by enemies:

Daniel CHOSE CHARACTER OVER COMFORT – to do the most with the situations he was handed, rather than complain about the ones he wasn't! (6:1-3)

Daniel 6:1 It seemed good to Darius to appoint 120 satraps over the kingdom, that they would be in charge of the whole kingdom, 2 and over them three commissioners (of whom Daniel was one), that these satraps might be accountable to them, and that the king might not suffer loss. 3 Then this Daniel began distinguishing himself among the commissioners and satraps because he possessed an extraordinary spirit, and the king planned to appoint him over the entire kingdom.

The fact is that Daniel wasn't where he would naturally have been, had it not been for the sins of his fathers and the captivity they caused. He could have sat in the corner and decided that "life dealt him a bad hand" – and therefore he would pout and be soured. His heart would have made him unusable to God if that were the case.

Let me ask you something: Is that what you are doing? Have you felt that the card hand God dealt you was somehow lacking, and because of that, you exempt yourself from looking at life in a positive way?

Daniel distinguished himself in a bad place, surrounded by some bad people. I know this because his marks of distinction brought out their jealousy a few verses later in this very story. What he remembered in life is an important lesson for all of us: **any test we face is more complicated than we may be led to believe.** When he faced challenges, they were NOT simply the test before him, but the test of what was INSIDE of him – what his walk with God in life truly was. Let me see if an illustration may shed light on this thought:

Dr. Madison Sarratt taught mathematics at Vanderbilt for many years. Before giving a test, he would put things in perspective for his students by admonishing his class with these words: "Today I am giving two examinations: one in trigonometry, and the other in honesty. I hope you will pass them both. But, if you must fail one, fail trigonometry. There are many good people in the world who cannot pass trigonometry, but there are no good people in the world who cannot pass the examination of honesty."

Many people seem to forget that external challenges have been approved by God to help us evaluate how true our walk is before Him. If we are not careful to be sensitive to obedience to God, we can easily learn in this life to "settle" for some level of dishonesty.

I am thinking of the man I heard about years ago who wrote to the IRS: "Dear Sirs, Last year when I filed my income tax return, I deliberately misrepresented my income. Now I cannot sleep. Enclosed is a check for $150 for taxes. If I still can't sleep, I will send the rest." (taken from sermoncentral.com illustrations).

Daniel chose character over comfort. He chose pushing himself instead of pouting about what he didn't have. That distinguished him – and it will distinguish you in life as well.

Daniel CHOSE DISCIPLINE OVER DISORDER – he did what he should have done and refused what to do what he shouldn't do. (6:4-9)

Daniel 6:4 Then the commissioners and satraps began trying to find a ground of accusation against Daniel in regard to government affairs; but they could find no ground of accusation or evidence of corruption, inasmuch as he was faithful, and no negligence or corruption was to be found in him. 5 Then these men said, "We will not find any ground of accusation against this Daniel unless we find it against him with regard to the law of his God." 6 Then these commissioners and satraps came by agreement to the king and spoke to him as follows: "King Darius, live forever! 7 All the commissioners of the kingdom, the prefects and the satraps, the high officials and the governors have consulted together that the king should establish a statute and enforce an injunction that anyone who makes a petition to any god or man besides you, O king, for thirty days, shall be cast into the lions' den. 8 Now, O king, establish the injunction and sign the document so that it may not be changed, according to the law of the Medes and Persians, which may not be revoked." 9 Therefore King Darius signed the document, that is, the injunction.

When I read this story, I was struck by the description of Daniel. I wondered how a group of enemies trying to trip me up would evaluate me. Go back to verse four and look carefully at what political reporters and party hacks found when they delved deeply into Daniel's private life…nothing. The description of FAITHFULNESS was vivid: "no ground for accusation," "no evidence of corruption," "no negligence"…WOW! That description meant that Daniel wasn't just NOT DOING WRONG, he was faithfully, diligently DOING RIGHT! Is that what my political opponents would say of me if I were in a government job as he was?

One of the things Daniel needed to bear in mind as he faced the simple tests of day to day living is that "someone is always watching."

Another lesson, equal to that one, helped him keep a positive attitude about life: challenges give me a platform to show my love and devotion to the Lord. They come into my life through the stamp of God's approval, because they help TEST ME so that God can show me where I am lacking in my preparation for His use.

I read somewhere years ago about eagles, and I confess I don't know wildlife well enough to know if what the author wrote was factual, but it was illustrative. He wrote:

A female eagle has an interesting way of picking a mate. She will pick up a twig, fly high into the air, and drop it. Male eagles will fly beneath her and try to catch the twig. She will do this until a male has caught the twig three times. The female is testing the male for his ability to catch young eagles as they are directed out of the nest for flight. When it's time for the young eagle to fly on its own, the mother eagle pushes her young out of the nest. She carries the young eaglets on her back up high into the air and shakes them off. It is the responsibility of the father to swoop down and catch the young eaglets until they learn to fly on their own. Just as the female eagle is testing the male for his reliability, God will test a believer in his or her faithfulness and dependability. Similarly, in our walk with God we often run into difficult situations that require us to make decisions. These decisions are clear indications to the Father whether or not we can be trusted to move ahead to the next level of responsibility. As the female eagle tests the male with twigs to determine which one would be her choice for a mate, God is testing us through daily decisions to determine which ones He can rely on to be used to build His kingdom. (*Twigs* by Chris Harken from Maple Grove, Minnesota USA)

Daniel chose to respond to life with discipline and tried to figure out how to best use his circumstances to honor God. When we do that, we will find that some of the tests open the doors to great opportunities…

Did you ever go walking through a field and get "stickers" poking you through your socks or your jeans? Did you ever get frustrated and think, "These must have come after the Fall of Man in the Garden!"

There is no way that God would make these for man, is there? One man saw them differently, and these "stickers" poking his skin changed his life...

In 1948, a Swiss mountaineer named George de Mestral was walking through the woods and was very frustrated by the burs that clung to his clothes. While picking them off, he realized that it may be possible to use this principle to make a fastener to compete with the zipper. Velcro was inspired by the natural sticking properties of burrs. If you look at a Velcro strip, you'll notice that it has two parts to it: a strip that has a web of tiny hooks; and a strip that has a web of tiny interwoven hoops. These two strips are a match for each other and when you join them together the hooks "catch" the loops and they become meshed together in a very strong bond. What makes Velcro important is the reliability in the many small strands that predictably stick together! (SOURCE: Darren Ethier, *The Velcro Effect*" on www.sermoncentral.com. Citation: The Useless Information Site, *ZIPPERS & VELCRO*)

Isn't it TELLING that George saw what everyone saw, but looked at it with different eyes? That is EXACTLY what Daniel did. He looked at life and decided to face it with discipline and discernment. He didn't just "look at the bright side of problems; **he worked through problems as PART of his walk with God.**"

If we spend our time fussing and blaming, we use up the energy that could be spent working through the issue and gaining from it. It takes DISCIPLINE to shut off the emotional flow, and become productive in spite of the temptation to wallow in self-pity and moan injustice. Emotional discipline is essential to godliness.

Daniel CHOSE LOVE OVER LIFE - he continued to follow hard after God and continued the prayers he normally made. (6:10-15)

Daniel 6:10 Now when Daniel knew that the document was signed, he entered his house (now in his roof chamber he had windows open toward Jerusalem); and he continued kneeling on his knees three times a day, praying and giving thanks before his God, as he had been doing previously. 11 Then these men came by agreement and found Daniel making petition and supplication before his God. 12 Then they approached and spoke before the king about the king's injunction, "Did you not sign an injunction that any man who makes a petition to any god or man besides you, O king, for thirty days, is to be cast into the lions' den?" The king replied, "The statement is true, according to the law of the Medes and Persians, which may not be revoked." 13 Then they answered and spoke before the king, "Daniel, who is one of the exiles from Judah, pays no attention to you, O king, or to the injunction which you signed, but keeps making his petition three times a day." 14 Then, as soon as the king heard this statement, he was deeply distressed and set his mind on delivering Daniel; and even until sunset he kept exerting himself to rescue him. 15 Then these men came by agreement to the king and said to the king, "Recognize, O king, that it is a law of the Medes and Persians that no injunction or statute which the king establishes may be changed."

I want you to look very closely at the age-old strategy of our spiritual enemy to shut off the influence of God's people in society – **because he is doing it again**. You must see not only the men who opposed Daniel of old, but also the strategy of the enemy behind them – the puppeteer of darkness.

When a believer walks uprightly, they are dangerous to the enemy.

- He assails them with temptation, and for many –that is enough to sideline them.

- If they succumb, they will waste energies fighting guilt that blocks them from truly experiencing God in daily life.

- When that DOESN'T WORK, the enemy may choose to drop into plan "B," and try a different approach – like "redrawing lines."

- What he often does is structure new laws to put the believer on the outside of civil obedience – forcing a confrontation due to societal standards that are changed.

Outlawing prayer in Daniel 6, five hundred years before Jesus, was a strategic form we see again emerging in a society that is trying to force believers to pay for abortions and to offer services to the abhorrence they call "same sex marriage." **The effort of the enemy of our souls is to redraw the lines of the law to move us outside of it – making the believer the "violator."** It is an old strategy for which Daniel faced a lion's den. Believers need to be aware of the enemy's strategic moves, because God uncovered them as such in His Word.

When Daniel knew the test was in place, his love for God drove him to continue praying! It wasn't an OPTION for him – it was his LIFE CONNECTION TO GOD!

Samuel Chadwick wrote: The one concern of the devil is to keep Christians from praying. He fears nothing from prayer-less studies, prayer-less work and prayer-less religion. He laughs at our toil, mocks at our wisdom, but he trembles when we pray. **Believers who look at prayer as a duty don't gaze at God in awe, or desire time with Him out of LOVE.**

It is essential that every believer recognize that love of the Lord must take precedence over love of things, and eventually of physical life itself.

Ken Walker writes in *Christian Reader* that in the 1995 college football season 6-foot-2-inch, 280-pound Clay Shiver, who played center for the Florida State Seminoles, was regarded as one of the best in the nation. In fact, one magazine wanted to name him to their preseason All-American football team. But that was a problem, because the magazine was *Playboy*, and Clay Shiver is a dedicated Christian. Shiver and the team chaplain suspected that Playboy would select him, and so he had time to prepare his response. Shiver knew well what a boon this could be for his career. Being chosen for this All-American team meant that sportswriters regarded him as the best in the nation at his position. Such publicity never hurts athletes who aspire to the pros and to multimillion-dollar contracts. But Shiver had higher values and priorities. When informed that *Playboy* had made their selection, Clay Shiver simply said, "No thanks." That's right; he flatly turned down the honor. Clay didn't want to embarrass his mother and grandmother by appearing in the magazine or giving old high school friends an excuse to buy that issue. Shiver further explained by quoting *Luke 12:48: "To whom much is given, of him much is required."* "I don't want to let anyone down," said Shiver, "and **number one on that list is God.**" (Larson, p. 53)

Let's face it, Daniel knew what continuing prayer would cost him, but prayer wasn't a RELIGIOUS activity, it was meeting with the God that he loved and lived for.

Daniel CHOSE POISE OVER PANIC – he knew his life was always preserved by God until the Lord was finished with him. (6:16-23)

Daniel 6:16 Then the king gave orders, and Daniel was brought in and cast into the lions' den. The king spoke and said to Daniel, "Your God whom you constantly serve will Himself deliver you." 17 A stone was brought and laid over the mouth of the den; and the king sealed it with his own signet ring and with the signet rings of his nobles, so that nothing would be changed in regard to Daniel. 18 Then the king went off to his palace and spent the night fasting, and no entertainment was brought before him; and his sleep fled from him. 19 Then the king arose at dawn, at the break of day, and went in haste to the lions' den. 20 When he had come near the den to Daniel, he cried out with a troubled voice. The king spoke and said to Daniel, "Daniel, servant of the living God, has your God, whom you constantly serve, been able to deliver you from the lions?" 21 Then Daniel spoke to the king, "O king, live forever! 22 "My God sent His angel and shut the lions' mouths and they have not harmed me, inasmuch as I was found innocent before Him; and also toward you, O king, I have committed no crime." 23 Then the king was very pleased and gave orders for Daniel to be taken up out of the den. So Daniel was taken up out of the den and no injury whatever was found on him, because he had trusted in his God.

The ending phrase of Daniel 6:23 makes clear the reason behind Daniel's choice – it wasn't compulsion or duty – it was **trust. He trusted God to do what God wanted done if he did what God instructed.** That is the essence of a surrendered life. He held his head high and knew the truth: We are invincible until God says our life has completed its mission.

In his book, *When God Whispers Your Name*, Max Lucado tells the story of John Egglen, who had never preached a sermon in his life before the Sunday morning when it snowed and the pastor wasn't able to make it to the church. In fact, he was the only deacon to show up. He was not a preacher, but he was faithful and that meant on that particular Sunday morning he preached. God rewarded his faithfulness, and at the end of his hesitant sermon, one young man invited God into his heart. No one there could appreciate the significance of what had taken place that morning. The young man who accepted Christ that snowy Sunday morning was none other than Charles Haddon Spurgeon, the man who has often been called, the "prince of preachers." God blessed his preaching and when he was still less than 30 years old he became the pastor of London's Metropolitan Tabernacle. His sermons were so powerful that although the building could hold 5000 people, the crowds who came to hear him were so thick that they would line up outside trying to hear his sermons. That amazing life of faith all started on a cold Sunday morning with the faithfulness of a deacon!

Trusting a God we cannot see is **not easy** when facing pain **we can feel**, and judgment we will physically discern. At the same time, if our faith means anything at all, it means the ability to be courageous with trust in the hands of a God Who is limitless in power!

Daniel CHOSE REST OVER REVENGE – he did not celebrate, nor encourage any harm against those who trapped him. (6:24-28)

Daniel 6:24 The king then gave orders, and they brought those men who had maliciously accused Daniel, and they cast them, their children and their wives into the lions' den; and they had not reached the bottom of the den before the lions overpowered them and crushed all their bones. 25 Then Darius the king wrote to all the peoples, nations and men of every language who were living in all the land: "May your peace abound! 26 I make a decree that in all the dominion of my kingdom men are to fear and tremble before the God of Daniel; for He is the living God and enduring forever and His kingdom is one that will not be destroyed, and His dominion will be forever. 27 He delivers and rescues and performs signs and wonders In Heaven and on Earth, Who has also delivered Daniel from the power of the lions." 28 So this Daniel enjoyed success in the reign of Darius and in the reign of Cyrus the Persian.

Nowhere in the text do you read of Daniel's delight as his plotting, conniving enemies became burnt toast. He made a choice to focus on God, not his adversaries. He knew the truth: Resting in the Lord will build us up inside!

The story is told of a persecuted Christian under Emperor Diocletian who was being chased by some soldiers under orders to put him to death. He saw a cave and rushed in to hide there. The soldiers arrived some time later. As they started to go in, they noticed a spider's web across the cave. They reasoned that no one had gone into that cave because the spider's web was there. Later on, the Christian came out and walked through the spider's web. He realized why the soldiers had not come in and said, "With God a web is as a wall. But without God a wall is as a spider's web." (A-Z Sermon Illustrations)

Daniel didn't know what he would experience in the lions' den but he knew that God would be with him. He put his trust in God, and rested in His goodness. He knew that where God led Him, God would stand with him – and that gave him rest. I think of a story:

A grandfather was out walking with his grandson one day. "How far do you think we are from home?" he asked the grandson. The boy said, "Grandpa, I don't know." The grandfather asked, "Well, where are you?" Again, the boy said, "I don't know." Then the grandfather chuckled and said, "Sounds to me as if you are lost." The young boy looked up at his grandfather and said, "**I can't be lost, I'm with you.**"

Daniel chose character over comfort.
He chose discipline over disorder.
He chose love for God over life without God.
He chose poise in the face of trouble over panic.
He chose rest over revenge.
He made choices that led him to positive peace… because:

Your ability to be positive has more to do with your life choices than your life circumstances!

Shine the Light
Lessons in Daniel

Lesson Seven: Daniel 2:19-45 "Revealing the Weakness"

It all started with a weak spot in the floor in the attic. A buddy and I were working on adding extra flooring over the joists that were already in place. Someone placed boards on the floor, but they were not sufficiently thick to hold anyone over one hundred pounds. We discovered this truth, quite by accident, when one of my friends stuck a foot all the way through to the dining room making his way across in the dark, looking for something in the attic. If we were looking for weakness, we found the perfect way to test for it – walk across the floor and see where we would fall through!

I wish every weakness in life could so easily be spotted. It seems like the times we live in are filled with people who have a weak strategy to navigate the flooring of life. Some people try to navigate life with emotions, but that seems to burn people out. Others try to get through by positive thinking, but that only works if your life isn't falling apart. Still others of our fellow citizens have decided the place to put their trust is in government to navigate the storms of life and care for their hopes and dreams of prosperity and stability. That may not be the best option, and it appears to be making many more dependent upon government services – at least according to some academic studies...Walter E. Williams, a professor of economics at George Mason University, wrote a column this week about the growing ranks of those classified as "poor" by the US Government's Census Bureau:

Here are a few facts about people whom the Census Bureau labels as "poor." Dr. Robert Rector and Rachel Sheffield, in their study … report that 80 percent of "poor" households have air conditioning; nearly three-quarters have a car or truck, and 31 percent have two or more. Two-thirds have cable or satellite TV. Half have one or more computers. Forty-two percent own their homes. "Poor" Americans have more living space (square footage) than the typical non-poor person in Sweden, France or the U.K. He paused in the report to add these words… "What we have in our nation are dependency and poverty of the spirit, with people making unwise choices and leading pathological lives aided and abetted by the welfare state…He went on to explain some things I had not calculated: Since President Lyndon Johnson declared war on poverty, the nation has spent about $18 trillion at the federal, state and local levels of government on programs justified by the "need" to deal with some aspect of poverty. In a column of mine in 1995, I pointed out that at that time, the nation had spent $5.4 trillion on the War on Poverty, and with that princely sum, "you could purchase every U.S. factory, all manufacturing equipment, and every office building. With what's left over, one could buy every airline, trucking company and our commercial maritime fleet. If you're still in the shopping mood, you could also buy every television, radio and power company, plus every retail and wholesale store in the entire nation." (http://tinyurl.com/kmhy6es) Today's total of $18 trillion spent on poverty means you could purchase everything produced in our country each year and then some.

I am no expert, but if what the report cites is true, the war on poverty is being won by poverty hands down – and that cannot make anyone feel good. This isn't a critique column on the poor, nor on the American government; it is a *Bible* lesson. Strangely, however, the theme of the verses we will study in this lesson are VERY MUCH about the weakness of trusting government, and several biblical reasons why you must not place your hope in its ability long term to meet your needs. The principle the text demonstrates clearly is this…

Key Principle: God is working a plan through kings and kingdoms (governments) – but human government won't ultimately fix what is broken – because it can't.

Let's go back into our study of Daniel... this time to look at the record of a specific prophecy. We studied the first six chapters in the book, but I deliberately side-stepped speaking on the passage at the end of chapter two, because the details of the prophecy fit better into the last part of the book, where we are going to detail each prophecy of the book and see if we can discern its interpretation based on what God gave us. Remember, the book is twelve chapters, with Daniel 1-6 a biographical and historical narrative (with the exception on 2:19-45), and Daniel 7-12 contains a series of prophetic records.

For teaching purposes, I would like to **split the text into two parts,** with the first part opening the door to our study of the prophetic portions of the whole book – by reminding us of **seven truths about prophecy** in Daniel 2:19-23.

Daniel 2:19 Then the mystery was revealed to Daniel in a night vision. Then Daniel blessed the God of Heaven; 20 Daniel said, "Let the name of God be blessed forever and ever, for wisdom and power belong to Him. 21 It is He who changes the times and the epochs; He removes kings and establishes kings; He gives wisdom to wise men and knowledge to men of understanding. 22 It is He Who reveals the profound and hidden things; He knows what is in the darkness, and the light dwells with Him. 23 To You, O God of my fathers, I give thanks and praise, for You have given me wisdom and power; even now You have made known to me what we requested of You, for You have made known to us the king's matter."

The seven truths are these:

God reveals what could not be known to man without His revelation of it – and that is a reason to PRAISE HIM.

Daniel 2:19 Then the mystery was revealed to Daniel in a night vision. Then Daniel blessed the God of Heaven.

Prophetic truth reminds us that God exists outside of TIME, and He is ABOVE AND BEYOND the plan of history.

Daniel 2: 20a Daniel said, "Let the name of God be blessed forever and ever..."

Prophecy illustrates the GREATNESS of God's mind, and His ABILITY to do what He promises.

Daniel 2:20b: "... For wisdom and power belong to Him."

Prophecy reminds us anew of God's SOVEREIGNTY over the universe.

Daniel 2:21a It is He Who changes the times and the epochs; He removes kings and establishes kings...

Prophecy humbles us, because even when we grasp its truths, we reckon it was not because of our own ability.

Daniel 2:21b ...He gives wisdom to wise men and knowledge to men of understanding.

It reminds us that what we cannot see is obvious to Him.

Daniel 2: 22 It is He Who reveals the profound and hidden things; He knows what is in the darkness, and the light dwells with Him.

Prophecy reminds us that understanding God's truth can only be achieved by prayer and dependence upon God.

Daniel 2: 23 To You, O God of my fathers, I give thanks and praise, for You have given me wisdom and power; even now You have made known to me what we requested of You, for You have made known to us the king's matter.

Stepping back and thinking through the verses, we easily recognize that we are in for "quite a ride" when we get involved in the prophetic portions of the Word.

First, we must acknowledge that GOD has to reveal truth – because we cannot fully grasp it without Him. Second, we must come to the conclusion that when **TRUTH is REVEALED** – it should lead us to **PRAISE GOD!**

With that short primer, off we go! The remaining verses in Daniel 2:24-45 contain **THREE simple parts**: the **setting** (Daniel 2:24-30), **what the king saw** (2:24-35) and **what God meant by it** (2:36-45). We will call the first part "the situation", the second part "the vision" and the third part "the lesson".

The Setting (Daniel 2:24-30)

The passage opens with a few verses of how Daniel got into the throne room to see the king. Normally, details like these would be at the edges of the narrative in terms of really helping us understand much about the prophecy – but there is a very important little lesson in the verses we dare not skip. Take a look.

Daniel 2:24 Therefore, Daniel went in to Arioch, whom the king had appointed to destroy the wise men of Babylon; he went and spoke to him as follows: "Do not destroy the wise men of Babylon! Take me into the king's presence, and I will declare the interpretation to the king." 25 Then Arioch hurriedly brought Daniel into the king's presence and spoke to him as follows: "I have found a man among the exiles from Judah who can make the interpretation known to the king!" 26 The king said to Daniel, whose name was Belteshazzar, "Are you able to make known to me the dream which I have seen and its interpretation?" 27 Daniel answered before the king and said, "As for the mystery about which the king has inquired, neither wise men, conjurers, magicians [nor] diviners are able to declare [it] to the king. 28 However, there is a God in Heaven Who reveals mysteries, and He has made known to King Nebuchadnezzar what will take place in the latter days. This was your dream and the visions in your mind [while] on your bed. 29 As for you, O king, [while] on your bed your thoughts turned to what would take place in the future; and He Who reveals mysteries has made known to you what will take place. 30 But as for me, this mystery has not been revealed to me for any wisdom residing in me more than [in] any [other] living man, but for the purpose of making the interpretation known to the king, and that you may understand the thoughts of your mind.

You can see **three important facts** are mentioned:

- **First,** Daniel and the other wise men faced death if the vision was not made plain (2:24-25).

- **Second,** Nebuchadnezzar was open to saving the men, but he wanted the vision made clear to him at all cost (2:26).

- **Third,** Daniel went to great length to make sure that it was ABSOLUTELY CLEAR that God could do what he could not do – and that God did not work BECAUSE of Daniel, but because of His Sovereign choice to reveal truth to men (2:27-30).

How significant it is for us to begin a study of prophetic portions **BATHED in the humility that God chooses to reveal truth to men** – not because of how GOOD they are, SMART they are, or even how WELL STUDIED they are. We should study hard – but that won't guarantee truth's revealing. God does what man cannot do. He speaks from the black darkness, where He can see every bit as clearly as if it were a place drenched in light. God is not blinded by time or circumstance. He alone knows all things, and He shares that which He chooses to share. We must not grow into arrogance from study of truth that He chooses to reveal – quite the opposite. We should feel smaller in His presence.

The Vision (Daniel 2:31-35)

As Daniel opened the imagery of the dream, he confirmed in the mind of the king that God was truly the speaker, for Daniel could not fake this detail. Daniel reported:

Daniel 2:31 You, O king, were looking and behold, there was a single great statue; that statue, which was large and of extraordinary splendor, was standing in front of you, and its appearance was awesome. 32 The head of that statue [was made] of fine gold, its breast and its arms of silver, its belly and its thighs of bronze, 33 its legs of iron, its feet partly of iron and partly of clay. 34 You continued looking until a stone was cut out without hands, and it struck the statue on its feet of iron and clay and crushed them. 35 Then the iron, the clay, the bronze, the silver and the gold were crushed all at the same time and became like chaff from the summer threshing floors; and the wind carried them away so that not a trace of them was found. But the stone that struck the statue became a great mountain and filled the whole Earth.

Daniel said the king's **vision had four parts:**

First, there was the **image or statue of a man**. The vast statue was in a human form and was considered "awesome" – perhaps a reference to its size (2:31). It was also clearly a made statue cast from different materials. Daniel scanned the view of the image from head to foot: The head was made of gold, the chest and arms were made of silver. The belly and mid-section were made of bronze, and the legs were made of iron. The feet were made of iron and hardened pottery (2:32-33).

Second, the king had observed the **formation of a ballista stone** that was cut without human hands and hurled without aid at the statue (2:34). The ballista crushed the statue from the foot to the head, crushing the image quickly into dust (2:35a).

Third, the **refuse pile of the statue that now lay crushed to dust**, was blown by a great wind – until the refuse disappeared (2:35b).

Fourth, the ballista stone grew into a **powerful mountain** that covered the surface of the Earth (2:35b).

It was essential for Daniel to move systematically through the vision to present the whole of the lesson, while confirming the details of the vision with the king. Yet, all this detail would not help the king, Daniel, or you and me – if it were not for the last part of the chapter… where Daniel was able to reveal the point of the revelation…

The Lesson (Daniel 2:36-45)

Daniel explained:

Daniel 2:36 This [was] the dream; now we will tell its interpretation before the king. 37 "You, O king, are the king of kings, to whom the God of Heaven has given the kingdom, the power, the strength and the glory; 38 and wherever the sons of men dwell, [or] the beasts of the field, or the birds of the sky, He has given [them] into your hand and has caused you to rule over them all. You are the head of gold.

Daniel made the simple point that Nebuchadnezzar was the gold head of the statue. He had what he had because God gave it to him – but he had MUCH. No question about it: the Babylonian king and his empire were the first part of the revelation... He continued:

Daniel 2:39 After you there will arise another kingdom inferior to you, then another third kingdom of bronze, which will rule over all the earth. 40 Then there will be a fourth kingdom as strong as iron; inasmuch as iron crushes and shatters all things, so, like iron that breaks in pieces, it will crush and break all these in pieces.

The fact that Babylon wasn't the LAST great kingdom was made clear. There would be another, then another, then another – each less valuable in their essence, but, in some ways, stronger in their power. Daniel didn't dwell on that truth, but that was implied in the different materials of each kingdom. Gold is very expensive, but very malleable. Silver may be valued as less – but it is a stronger metal. Bronze is certainly stronger than silver or gold, and iron stronger than all. Yet NONE OF THE KINGDOMS will be strong enough to resist the ballista stone's eventual crushing work. Before he fully explained the interpretation, Daniel got distracted by the feet. God wanted to say something about the FEET:

Daniel 2:41 In that you saw the feet and toes, partly of potter's clay and partly of iron, it will be a divided kingdom; but it will have in it the toughness of iron, inasmuch as you saw the iron mixed with common clay. 42 [As] the toes of the feet [were] partly of iron and partly of pottery, [so] some of the kingdom will be strong and part of it will be brittle. 43 And in that you saw the iron mixed with common clay, they will combine with one another in the seed of men; but they will not adhere to one another, even as iron does not combine with pottery.

The feet seemed to be a REVIVAL of the legs in a slightly different form. The legs were NOT EXACTLY like the feet – because the feet were made from mixed materials. If each material represented a DIFFERENT KINGDOM – it is clear the fourth kingdom had both an iron phase, and a mixed phase that followed it. Since the kingdoms can be identified now with Babylon, Medo-Persia, Greece and Rome – the feet seem to be a revival of Roman-like government that is made a bit differently. Let me suggest the clear difference is that the legs were ONE PEOPLE, while the feet were men and women from DIFFERENT NATIONS that joined in a Senate-like republic that drew men from many places. Let me further point out that it was not a "melting pot" – but rather a coalition of people that included both COMMON MEN and those of significance.

I don't believe it would be a stretch to project the feet as a republic that dominated the world at the end time – before God steps in to end governments of men with a powerful blow from Heaven. It includes people who TRY TO STAY TOGETHER in a coalition – but they cannot. They are TOO DIFFERENT! Look at Daniel's commentary as he continued:

Daniel 2:44 In the days of those kings the God of heaven will set up a kingdom which will never be destroyed, and [that] kingdom will not be left for another people; it will crush and put an end to all these kingdoms, but it will itself endure forever. 45 Inasmuch as you saw that a stone was cut out of the mountain without hands and that it crushed the iron, the bronze, the clay, the silver and the gold, the great God has made known to the king what will take place in the future; so the dream is true and its interpretation is trustworthy.

This was the point of the vision Nebuchadnezzar had in the first place. God will **PUT AN END TO HUMAN GOVERNMENT**. Men won't end in chaos by their own choosing – God will crush government and take over direct control of the scene Himself. Later on, we will discover the *Bible* projects the coming of Messiah as a JUDGE. Jesus said it clearly:

Matthew 25:31 But when the Son of Man comes in His glory, and all the angels with Him, then He will sit on His glorious throne. 32 All the nations will be gathered before Him; and He will separate them from one another, as the shepherd separates the sheep from the goats; 33 and He will put the sheep on His right, and the goats on the left. 34 Then the King will say to those on His right, 'Come, you who are blessed of My Father, inherit the kingdom prepared for you from the foundation of the world... 41 Then He will also say to those on His left,' Depart from Me, accursed ones, into the eternal fire which has been prepared for the devil and his angels...' 46 These will go away into eternal punishment, but the righteous into eternal life.

The simple fact of the matter is that a judge is coming – but He is a perfect judge. He is coming to a world that is not prepared, and to believers that should be prepared. The *Bible* teaches that he is not going to offer eternal judgment to followers of Jesus because of their sin – for that was fully judged at the Cross and our trust in the work of Jesus alone covers us from any future penalty for our sin. The lamb paid for all of our sin. God has been clear. At the same time, the performance as a believer is going to be judged when the Savior comes – and I should walk every day with that coming review in mind. Let me show it to you in the context of the seventh trumpet in Revelation 11:

Revelation 11:15 Then the seventh angel sounded; and there were loud voices in Heaven, saying, "The kingdom of the world has become the kingdom of our Lord and of His Christ; and He will reign forever and ever." 16 And the twenty-four elders, who sit on their thrones before God, fell on their faces and worshiped God, 17 saying, "We give You thanks, O Lord God, the Almighty, Who are and Who were, because You have taken Your great power and have begun to reign. 18 And the nations were enraged, and Your wrath came, and the time came for the dead to be judged, and the time to reward Your bond-servants the prophets and the saints and those who fear Your name, the small and the great, and to destroy those who destroy the Earth."

As I told you when we studied the details of Revelation 11: When I stand before Jesus – seconds, minutes, hours, days, weeks, months and years will evaporate into the smoke as the fire of His eyes burn through my life's work. What is left after all the selfish, ego-driven, stubborn, hard-hearted, gossip-laden, flesh-colored work is gone – is what Jesus can BEGIN to celebrate. Mature believers keep that day in their minds eye – and never lose sight of it. Brethren, some of us seem to be content wasting our only opportunity to please Him!

Yet, **here is the point of our lesson: Government is a temporary tool from the Master's tool box**. Like bodily exercise, it profits SOME and for a TIME – but it is NOT THE ANSWER to humanity's needs.

God is working a plan through kings and kingdoms (governments) – but human government won't ultimately fix what is broken – because it can't. Nebuchadnezzar got the opportunity to see it clearly! Look at the end of the passage in Daniel 2:

Daniel 2:46 Then King Nebuchadnezzar fell on his face and did homage to Daniel, and gave orders to present to him an offering and fragrant incense. 47 The king answered Daniel and said, "Surely your God is a God of gods and a Lord of kings and a revealer of mysteries, since you have been able to reveal this mystery." 48 Then the king promoted Daniel and gave him many great gifts, and he made him ruler over the whole province of Babylon and chief prefect over all the wise men of Babylon. 49 And Daniel made request of the king, and he appointed Shadrach, Meshach and Abed-nego over the administration of the province of Babylon, while Daniel [was] at the king's court.

The end of the passage was **God using government to promote His men and His agenda.** That is what it can do if God is revered. That is the BEST it can do – but it must be willing to follow Him!

Look at the truths:

- God's kingdom begins to rise while the other earthly kingdoms are still operating (2:44a).

- God does the work of bringing His kingdom to men (2:44b).

- God's kingdom is NEVER destroyed, NEVER overthrown, NEVER bankrupt, NEVER mismanaged, NEVER vanquished, and NEVER ends (2:44b).

- God's kingdom CRUSHES all men's efforts to build a lasting peace and prosperity through governments made by their own hands (2:44b).

- God brings about God's government Himself – it is NOT a work of men (2:45).

Finally, we must remember the whole picture:

- **God will allow human government – until He is done with it.**
- **God will invite men to unite and participate – but they will fail.**
- **God will replace human government with a perfect King and peaceful kingdom.**

Christ shall reign. He will not reign from WITHIN human government – He will CRUSH human government and reign in its place. It will be as David reigned – a Sovereign over a people. This is no reflection of a spiritual reign through a church in a world system that does not love Him, and countries that do not obey Him. **Christ shall reign - forever and ever.**

Are you ready to have Him as your king?

Shine the Light
Lessons in Daniel

Lesson Eight: Daniel 7:1-28 "Facing a Nightmare"

Did you ever feel like the COWARDLY LION? I had a nightmare the other morning, and it startled me. I was asked to speak at a new building that our church just somehow took over, but I lost my notes, my ironed shirt, my car keys, and the iPad I use for my *Bible*. I was running around the building and the people were not you – they were all different people, and NONE of them seemed to want to help me find my way to my things, and then to the pulpit of this labyrinth style church building. The rooms wound one into another, and I felt frustrated and hopelessly lost... I was unnerved, unsure, unprepared, and about to become unglued. For me, that was a nightmare. I awoke and prayed that I would have not only my messages ready, but my heart as well, so that I might speak for the Lord with both His heart, and the tenor of His voice.

Did you ever have a terrible nightmare that came back to you even after you awoke? A nightmare can be so thoroughly engaging that you can be CONVINCED you are truly living it, or you may even be able to discern that it is not real, but rather a dream state (even while it is ongoing).

Web MD explains: Nightmares are vividly realistic; disturbing dreams that rattle you awake from a deep sleep. ... Because periods of REM sleep become progressively longer as the night progresses, you may find you experience nightmares most often in the early morning hours.

Doctors aren't completely sure what triggers them, but they offered these thoughts in the same source: Nightmares in adults are often spontaneous, but they can also be caused by a variety of factors and underlying disorders. Some people have nightmares after having a late-night snack, which can increase metabolism and signal the brain to be more active. ...

Hmm.... **Now I am trying to recall what I ate before I went to bed the other night**... As riveting as the story of my personal sleep disorders may be, I didn't come to share my story today, but rather my Master's story. Strangely enough, our lesson will be taken from an inspired nightmare. **God delivered a message to the prophet Daniel through a nightmare – and it left him troubled and pale.** Then God let him do something that was incredibly helpful... He wrote it down for us. He shared it for the generations that followed his ministry, and we have it today. God spoke to Daniel in a way that Daniel would understand – dreams. He had already established, years before under the Babylonian King Nebuchadnezzar II that God worked through him in that way – so God used it in his later life personally.

Key Principle: When God wants to reveal something, He has many options, and all of them will seem invasive if we don't know, love, and trust Him.

Daniel DID know God – but even in that state, this was a powerfully difficult message to receive from God... a message about long centuries of godless rulers and powerful pagans that would follow their PASSION FOR POWER rather than an opportunity to PROMOTE THEIR CREATOR. The message scared Daniel, but it wasn't given to hurt him. Truth can hurt, but that isn't its original intention much of the time. This painful truth became clear to Daniel...

God has a purpose for telling the story of Who He is in human history, but when injustice is allowed to run rampant in the streets, no believer is immune from feeling the swell of the question inside: "God, why don't You DO something about this?" Habakkuk cried out his question to God in the face of injustice... it was unbearable. Daniel's vision was simple: wicked king after wicked king would rule and do wrong – all as part of God's unfolding drama of human history. It upset Daniel, and it upsets us. I HATE that evil men seem to prevail in so many world conflicts. It is hard not to be beat down by it all! If you have ever felt that, you understand the heart behind the record in chapter seven of Daniel.

It is worth noting that this vision (the second after the one recorded in chapter 2:19-45) was maintained in the ancient manuscript in Aramaic, not Hebrew – so it seems this lesson was for the world of Daniel's day (and the rulers) to easily comprehend. God wasn't embarrassed the evil would appear to prevail with such power and unchecked determination.

Sometimes people who are critical of God's people and God's Word, like to use their seemingly enduring power as evidence of their supremacy, a sort of "might makes right" idea. God included in the text the truth that men who HATE God and His people will have their centuries to rule, but they would not ultimately last... God will end all things in righteousness, firmly held in His control. This is His plan and it was disturbing before he settled into God's message. Take a look:

First, consider the situation (7:1).

7:1 In the first year of Belshazzar king of Babylon Daniel saw a dream and visions in his mind as he lay on his bed; then he wrote the dream down and related the following summary of it.

Belshazzar was the son of Nabonidus, who ruled three years and then left his throne to his son while he devoted himself to the worship of the moon god Sin in a desert oasis – a spiritual pilgrimage of sorts. Belshazzar became co-regent in 553 BCE, and was supposed to attend to Babylon's defense during his dad's journey. A few years later, in about 540 BCE, Nabonidus returned when he heard the Persians planned to take the city of Babylon from his son. Nabonidus marched to face Cyrus the Mede, but was defeated and on October 10, 539 BCE, he surrendered to Cyrus. Two days later the Persian armies overthrew the haughty city of Babylon that was engaged in a drunken party as Daniel recorded in our earlier lesson on Daniel 5.

The point of this statement was to share that Belshazzar was a new prince. The young man was new at the job, and as we have seen in a previous lesson, his passions led him. He wasn't a strong moral ruler, nor did he appear in historical record as a deeply spiritual or reflective man. I cannot prove it, but I have an idea that the prince's actions in the throne room and banquet hall may have been part of what fed Daniel a nightmare. Daniel evidently wrote the dream to explain the matters within it. The "kept in my heart" reference of 7:28 may refer to his reactions only - it is unclear. What is clear is that the nightmare was painful to behold and scary to contemplate, and then he awoke to Prince "Party Animal the Selfish." These were days when Daniel really may have questioned what in the world he was doing on this divine assignment. Did you ever do that?

Second, beyond the "situation" that was playing out, by his record Daniel allows us to consider the elements of the vision (7:2-8).

7:2 Daniel said, "I was looking in my vision by night, and behold, the four winds of heaven were stirring up the great sea. ³ And four great beasts were coming up from the sea, different from one another. ⁴ The first was like a lion and had the wings of an eagle. I kept looking until its wings were plucked, and it was lifted up from the ground and made to stand on two feet like a man; a human mind also was given to it. ⁵ And behold, another beast, a second one, resembling a bear. And it was raised up on one side, and three ribs were in its mouth between its teeth; and thus they said to it, 'Arise, devour much meat! **⁶** *After this, I kept looking, and behold, another one, like a leopard, which had on its back four wings of a bird; the beast also had four heads, and dominion was given to it.* **⁷** *After this I kept looking in the night visions, and behold, a fourth beast, dreadful and terrifying and extremely strong; and it had large iron teeth. It devoured and crushed and trampled down the remainder with its feet; and it was different from all the beasts that were before it, and it had ten horns.* **⁸** *While I was contemplating the horns, behold, another horn, a little one, came up among them, and three of the first horns were pulled out by the roots before it; and behold,* ᶠ*this horn possessed eyes like the eyes of a man and a mouth uttering great boasts.*

Essentially, he saw four beasts (7:4-8). Each beast, according to verse 17 represented kings and their kingdoms. Perhaps the dream sounds strange to you, picturing different kingdoms by specific animals. Yet, think about it... around the world we use symbols of our country relating to a bald eagle. Let's see if there are any of the nations on the list of four above that make sense to us:

First, there was a kingdom that is pictured by a lion with wings.

Assyrian, Babylonian and Persian rulers all loved lions. Years before this prophecy King Ashurbanipal II (850's BCE), had two 15 ton lions of war carved and placed at the entrance of the temple adjacent to his palace in the Assyrian capital of his day. Each lion was 2.25 meters wide and 2.6 meters high! One was recovered, discovered by Henry Layard in 1849 and is now located in the British Museum collection. Persians made royal lion hunts a part of their national pride symbolism. The king of the jungle is a natural for such symbolism. At the same time, none of us has seen lions with wings...unless we traveled to ancient Persia. Such representations are found in Babylon, and all of the Persian Gulf. A lion with wings could easily befit Babylon because she was so swift in conquest of other kingdoms (cp. Jer. 49:22; Lam 4:19; Ezek. 17:3; Hab. 1:6, 8). Like in Daniel 2:19ff, the first kingdom is that of Babylon. It was formerly represented in the Daniel 2 vision as the head of gold.

Second, there was a kingdom pictured as a tilted bear with three ribs hanging from its mouth.

Like the arms and breast of silver from Daniel 2:32, the second kingdom seemed always to be a confederation of TWO THINGS. In the earlier vision, it was two arms crossed on the chest, and in this one, it is the lopsided bear. The Medes and Persians were such an empire, unequal partners in confederation – and their king, Cyrus, gobbled up several important cities on their way to taking Babylon as their prize. It is worth noting that early on, it appears that Median influence dominated during the reigns of Cyrus and Cambyses...but in time there appears to have been a drift more toward Persian dominance by the time of Xerxes fifty years later (some suggest that in the phrase from Esther 1:19, "the laws of the Persians and the Medes").

Third, there was a kingdom pictured as a leopard with four heads and four wings.

Greece followed Persia, and the detailed history of the exploits of Alexander the Great's chasing of Darius III are well known to historians. The leopard corresponds to the "belly and...thighs of bronze" from Daniel 2:32 and 39 – this time the emphasis being placed on the swiftness of the conquests. The four heads, no doubt, refer to the four Diadoche – the generals that took over after the untimely death of Alexander.

Donald Campbell adds: The expression "dominion was given to it" is most interesting and significant. Did Alexander imagine that it was his military genius alone that enabled him and his small army of 35,000 men to defeat the massive hordes of the Persians numbering, some believe, in the millions? It is true that Alexander was a great leader, but his victories and subsequent dominion over a great empire were his because God, in the execution of His plans, allowed it to happen. Will world rulers ever understand this important fact?" (Donald K Campbell, *Daniel: God's Man in a Secular Society.*)

Fourth, there was a kingdom pictured as a terrible monster with ten horns protruding from its head.

Before Daniel saw the last beast, the phrase "after that" may refer only to the sequence of the vision, but appears to suggest the order of the kingdoms themselves. Daniel had no way to make sense of this part of the vision from the animal world. It was a beast beyond his experience. Like the hard to describe "iron kingdom" we encountered earlier in Daniel 2:40 – this "terrible beast" was a different kind of kingdom. It appeared to be a conglomerate of things – not one cohesive thing. Finding Rome in this place is not at all difficult, for the might of that empire stretched from Scotland to Saudi Arabia and changed the face of the world for centuries. Their warfare and killing machinery was without parallel, and the vision made that clear.

Like the end of the Daniel 2 where the vision had ten toes, so the end of this vision had ten horns. They came out of the system of the fourth kingdom, but seemed to be an interesting separate detail from that system. Look back at the way Daniel was distracted by the horns:

7:7b ...it was different from all the beasts that were before it, and it had ten horns. 8 While I was contemplating the horns, behold, another horn, a little one, came up among them, and three of the first horns were pulled out by the roots before it; and behold, this horn possessed eyes like the eyes of a man and a mouth uttering great boasts.

The "ten horns" as a specific designation can be seen nine times in Scripture – three in Daniel 7 and six in Revelation 13 and 17. In this passage, it is interesting to note the ten horns refers to a singular kingdom grammatically in Aramaic, which implies that it is a divided single confederation composed of ten rulers, or that there are ten rulers in sequence. The real distraction was the BIG MOUTH on the LITTLE HORN at the end of verse eight.

Now step back for a second, and look at what Daniel recorded. He saw four kingdoms, and the last one had a complicated ending to it – with a variety of rulers and one really boastful individual that couldn't keep his mouth shut.

Babylon would give way to Persia, and Persia would succumb to Greece. The four Diadoche Kingdoms of Greece would be crushed by the iron treads of Rome. Rome would set a pattern that would build a coalition of ten kings, and a boastful and arrogant politician would arise on the world stage.

Prophecy students LOVE to get tied in the details, but that wasn't the point of the story – not really.

The third section of the story drew in the movement in Heaven (7:9-14).

One of only a few glimpses the Scriptures give us into the throne room of Heaven is found here. There are some striking similarities (as well as a few differences) from this description and the one found in Revelation 4 and 5! Hold on tight, because we are about to pull the curtain back to the very place where God dwells. The physical description represents an unfathomable spiritual world...

7:9: I kept looking until thrones were set up, and the Ancient of Days took His seat; His vesture was like white snow and the hair of His head like pure wool. His throne was ablaze with flames; its wheels were a burning fire. 10 A river of fire was flowing and coming out from before Him; thousands upon thousands were attending Him, and myriads upon myriads were standing before Him; the court sat, and the books were opened. 11 Then I kept looking because of the sound of the boastful words which the horn was speaking. I kept looking until the beast was slain, and its body was destroyed and given to the burning fire. 12 As for the rest of the beasts, their dominion was taken away, but an extension of life was granted to them for an appointed period of time. 13 I kept looking in the night visions, and behold, with the clouds of Heaven One like a Son of Man was coming, and He came up to the Ancient of Days and was presented before Him. 14 And to Him was given dominion, glory, and a kingdom that all the peoples, nations and men of every language might serve Him. His dominion is an everlasting dominion which will not pass away; and His kingdom is one which will not be destroyed.

Daniel's eyes were moved from the boasting horn by a much more impressive vision... that of God's throne room in Heaven. Think of what he saw! Many thrones were staged as the court of Heaven began to form before him. The Most High God sat down on the highest throne. His visage was beyond compare and his throne was like a moving chariot – with wheels beheld also by the prophet Ezekiel. Look at the God that you serve:

- He is seated on the throne as Judge of all things. Many have opinions, but none is His equal. He is uniquely qualified to discern all things.

- He is clothed in pure white, untainted, unstained, utterly distinct above all. None can compare to the shine of His purity. He is without spot, without blemish, without shadow of turning.

- The hair of His head is white as one with the vast wisdom of all the ages.

- The throne on which he sat was ablaze with a smelter's fire – for no dross or impurity would ever touch His holy personage.

- His throne was not stationary, but moving and flexible – engaged and ever nimble.

- A flow of fire came from that throne – the heat of holiness combined with the light of truth.

- Thousands of thousands attended Him – all Heaven attentive to His moves and commands.

Don't forget in all the familiarity of our day that God is not like us. He is not simply our heavenly buddy or spiritual chum... **He is King above all, Majestic and Holy, to be revered, worshiped and adored.** There is none like Him!

Ah, this is the special blessing of this passage, but it is ALSO THE PROBLEM OF THE PASSAGE. Look at Daniel's response in 7:15: *As for me, Daniel, my spirit was distressed within me, and the visions in my mind kept alarming me.*

Why was Daniel troubles? Why didn't the sight of Heaven COMFORT him? Because he could see the truth about what God was going to do... and the truth wasn't pleasant to behold! Keep reading... To understand, first look at the interpretation of the vision as it was explained first TO him, and , then BY him for us.

7:16: I approached one of those who were standing by and began asking him the exact meaning of all this. So he told me and made known to me the interpretation of these things: 17 'These great beasts, which are four in number, are four kings who will arise from the earth. 18 But the saints of the Highest One will receive the kingdom and possess the kingdom forever, for all ages to come.' 19 Then I desired to know the exact meaning of the fourth beast, which was different from all the others, exceedingly dreadful, with its teeth of iron and its claws of bronze, and which devoured, crushed and trampled down the remainder with its feet, 20 and the meaning of the ten horns that were on its head and the other horn which came up, and before which three of them fell, namely, that horn which had eyes and a mouth uttering great boasts and which was larger in appearance than its associates. 21 I kept looking, and that horn was waging war with the saints and overpowering them 22 until the Ancient of Days came and judgment was passed in favor of the saints of the Highest One, and the time arrived when the saints took possession of the kingdom. 23 "Thus he said: 'The fourth beast will be a fourth kingdom on the Earth, which will be different from all the other kingdoms and will devour the whole Earth and tread it down and crush it. 24 As for the ten horns, out of this kingdom ten kings will arise; and another will arise after them, and he will be different from the previous ones and will subdue three kings. 25 He will speak out against the Most High and wear down the saints of the Highest One, and he will intend to make alterations in times and in law; and they will be given into his hand for a time, times, and half a time. 26 But the court will sit for judgment, and his dominion will be taken away, annihilated and destroyed forever. 27 Then the sovereignty, the dominion and the greatness of all the kingdoms under the whole heaven will be given to the people of the saints of the Highest One; His kingdom will be an everlasting kingdom, and all the dominions will serve and obey Him.'

This isn't difficult to grasp. Look at the sequence:

- There will be four kings and respective kingdoms.
- The last one will have a renewed confederation with ten kings.
- There will arise an especially boastful big mouth – what a shock that politicians could be described that way!
- The big mouth took on God's people and really whipped them badly until God stepped in.
- Tuning in to the fourth kingdom – it would take over the planet and make a confederation of the world's rulers for a time.

Look even closer into verses 24-26, because it described in detail a specific period toward the end of all human history:

- Ten kings confederate, and AFTER THEM one arises that knocks out three other leaders.
- His boasting includes defiant blasphemy against God.
- His acts are against God's people, and he changes the order – redraws the calendar and changes the laws to conform to his own standards.
- He is cut off. His power is taken away. Heaven acts.
- The Kingdom God replaces the boastful one's rule with is the EVERLASTING KINGDOM.

Now, here is the statement of Daniel's feeling, yet again…Daniel *7:28 At this point the revelation ended. As for me, Daniel, my thoughts were greatly alarming me and my face grew pale, but I kept the matter to myself."*

The point of the story…

We have walked through details of kingdoms, but I cannot shake that Daniel is upset. Kings and kingdoms will rise and fall. Armies will march one against another in succession. Bad men will sit atop the pinnacle of power, only to be unseated by other bad men. Evil will reign for generations. God's people will suffer. Right will be trampled. Fair judgments will be overturned. Votes will be upended by a few who will force the rest of us into their twisted views of what they want. We will watch injustice, and we will feel powerless. We will want to give up. We will want to withdraw. We will feel like there is NO POINT…and we will be WRONG when we think that way. It won't end in injustice. God isn't abandoning mankind. It is true…

The struggle for a righteous kingdom will continue until God establishes His kingdom on Earth in place of the works of men.

- Should I flee to a monastery?
- Should I complain at the Heavens?
- Should I look for hope in the next politician to save us?
- Should I weep and cry, and feel that God has left the scene?

Not at all

- I should follow him.
- I should follow Him where He leads and boldly proclaim WHAT He says.
- I don't need to MAKE A DIFFERENCE.
- I need to be OBEDIENT.

Let me close with a story that may help illustrate what I am saying… Theodorot was a fourth century bishop from Syria, and he wrote a number of commentaries and stories. One of them was the incredible story of a monk named Telemachus…President Ronald Reagan told the story at a Prayer Breakfast in 1984, and since he was a better story teller than I will ever be, I will just quote his version:

[There was a] monk living in a little remote village, spending most of his time in prayer or tending the garden from which he obtained his sustenance – [his name was] Telemachus, [he lived] back in the fourth century. Then one day, he thought he heard the voice of God telling him to go to Rome, and believing that he had heard, he set out. Weeks and weeks later, he arrived there, having traveled most of the way on foot. It was at a time of a festival in Rome. They were celebrating a triumph over the Goths, and he followed a crowd into the Coliseum, and then there in the midst of this great crowd, he saw the gladiators come forth, stand before the Emperor, and say, "We who are about to die salute you." He realized they were going to fight to the death for the entertainment of the crowds. He cried out, "In the name of Christ, stop!" and his voice was lost in the tumult there in the great Coliseum. As the games began, he made his way down through the crowd, climbed over the wall and dropped to the floor of the arena. Suddenly the crowds saw this scrawny little figure making his way out to the gladiators and saying, over and over again, "In the name of Christ, stop." They thought it was part of the entertainment, and at first, they were amused. Then, when they realized it wasn't, they grew belligerent and angry. As he was pleading with the gladiators, "In the name of Christ, stop," one of them plunged his sword into his body, and as he fell to the sand of the arena in death, his last words were, "In the name of Christ, stop." Suddenly, a strange thing happened. The gladiators stood looking at this tiny form lying in the sand. A silence fell over the Coliseum. Then, someplace up in the upper tiers, an individual made his way to an exit and left, and others began to follow. In the dead silence, everyone left the Coliseum. That was the last battle to the death between gladiators in the Roman Coliseum. Never again, did anyone kill or did men kill each other for the entertainment of the crowd. One tiny voice that could hardly be heard above the tumult, "In the name of Christ, stop."

You don't know what your voice will do. You follow God. You don't follow Him only when it is fair and things are going well. You follow Him and do His bidding in your office, in your shop, in your carpool, in your home. You follow, and He will bring the end in His time. Injustice may prevail for a time. Sin may rage in our streets, but Heaven isn't slack concerning God's promises. God isn't impotent; He is patient. When it hurts, keep your eyes fixed on the eastern sky – your redemption draws near!

The struggle for a righteous kingdom will continue until God establishes His kingdom on Earth in place of the works of men.

Lessons in Daniel: Shine the Light

Shine the light
Lessons in Daniel

Lesson Nine: Daniel 8:1-27 "Seeing with New Eyes"

I don't often do this, but I want to begin on a very frank, but very negative note. Don't get worried, I have a purpose in mind…Let's be honest. It doesn't take much observation of evil on the news to make a believer feel sick. We can so easily become indignant when we watch the movement of evil in our time – and we have had to face it many, many times. Most of us feel a sense of moral collapse in the society around us – and it makes us at least mad, and at worse physically ill. Did you ever look at the sickness of our world and really question Heaven? Have you ever thought: "God, why don't You stop this? Why do You let these terrible things go on?"

No, I am not depressed, and I am not grumpy. The fact is that I am certain most of us have asked the question, and often we find ourselves not really grasping the answer – but that ISN'T BECAUSE GOD HASN'T GIVEN ONE.

Here is the truth: God is often at work in ways we don't recognize when evil seems to be collapsing the bulkheads of our society. He seems like He is "letting evil get away with things" when that isn't really what is going on at all. That is what it APPEARS, but that is not WHAT IT IS. Heaven is more subtle than Earth, and God more restrained in His work than most learn to see.

Let me show you an example of that truth from God's Word. Go back in time to ancient Babylon, and join the Jews in captivity. God was on the move, and showed His selected Prime Ministerial prophet the future of evil domination and pagan revelry against God – but even the veteran believer named Daniel couldn't really grasp it, and didn't like what God was doing. Before you read the passage, look at the end of the chapter. It simply says:

Daniel 8:26: "The vision of the evenings and mornings which has been told is true; but keep the vision secret, For [it] pertains to many days [in the future]." 27 Then I, Daniel, was exhausted and sick for days. Then I got up [again] and carried on the king's business; but I was astounded at the vision, and there was none to explain [it].

Did you see the reactive word: "exhausted"… "sick for days,"…"astounded"… Is that the reaction you would THINK a prophet would get from God exposing the future of things to him? The vision we are about to see is from two years AFTER the one we looked in in the chapter before it (Daniel 7). I want to remind you of the end of that last vision to set the theme of our lesson today. Look at how that one ended.

Daniel 7:28 At this point the revelation ended. As for me, Daniel, my thoughts were greatly alarming me, and my face grew pale, but I kept the matter to myself.

Unless he was deliberately trying to get his heart rate up, or lose some color in his cheeks, these prophecies don't seem to be drawing Daniel into warm and fuzzy feelings about God and His work among men! **Sometimes we think that if we UNDERSTOOD more of what was going to happen, if we could clearly see the prophetic truth of what lay ahead – we would be MORE CONTENT**. That doesn't seem to be true. Daniel saw ahead. God uncovered future truth to him – and it made him SICK. Why? It made him sick for the same reason that injustice viewed in today's news **MAKES US SICK**!

Like us, Daniel was tempted to fight the wrong battle – the one that captures the culture of his day with moral behavior, rather than a work that excitedly shares the truth of the existence of the spiritual world and God at work. Daniel learned that not only did he not WANT to see God's tolerance of evil in the world, but that God's patience made him physically ill. Yet, Daniel couldn't see what God saw…

Key Principle: The mature believer's view of the world should not be about the grasp of darkness, but rather about God at work – moving history toward His purposes.

Before we jump into a complicated prophetic scheme – let me say it plainly. **Even the most mature believers are too easily focused on the wrong things. We are distracted by the site of the march of pagans and immorality – and we don't recognize what God is doing through the darkness of men to bring His eventual and certain victory.** I don't want to spoil the message by tipping my hand too soon, but consider that what Daniel saw was not what God was trying to say – and that is why he got sick.

Daniel's visions of chapter two and chapter seven were about four pagan and powerful political systems – Babylon, Medo-Persia, Greece and Rome. Each had all the requisite characteristics of a government: inequity, inefficiency, graft, and corruption, etc. In the first vision, the four were revealed in a big statue that was made of different metals from head to toes. In the second vision, four beasts represented the four kingdoms. Stepping away from both, Daniel learned that GOD WAS GOING TO TOLERATE MUCH in the kingdoms of this world, and He even intended that damage be allowed against His own people in the process. That sickened Daniel, because he couldn't see the REASONS BEHIND WHAT GOD WAS DOING.

Let me crack that door open on just a few of the things God would do…

- **Daniel saw a Persian kingdom overthrowing the Babylonian Empire**... but God was going to use a Persian king to finally rid the Hebrews of an ancient Amalekite enemy from the family of Agag by unfolding a plot by Haman as recorded in the book of Esther. God was going to fulfill a prophecy given to Moses, through a girl named Hadassah (Esther) under a Persian King named Xerxes.

- **Daniel saw the despotism of Persian kings over the Jewish people**... but God was going to elevate and educate the Jewish people through the terror and threat of a Persian edict. The threat against their lives became the landscape of learning to take God seriously.

- **Daniel saw the rise of a swift pagan ruler of Macedonia (Greece) infecting the west with pagan philosophy and immorality**... but God was going to use the life of Alexander the Great to unify the Mediterranean world– giving a common bond of Greek to allow the Gospel to flow across the Mediterranean in due time.

- **Daniel saw a Greek dictator who exercised power relentlessly** – even inserting himself into ancient cultures and building pagan cities... but God was going to use the academy of Alexandria, a city founded by Alexander the Great, to produce the LXX translation of the *Hebrew Bible* – allowing the truth of God to move out to the world. **God was seeding the ground for the message of Jesus – but that was hard to see.**

God is often at work in ways we don't recognize when evil seems to be collapsing the bulkheads of our society.

Step back in time with me, and let's see if we can identify **what Daniel learned** from this, his third vision...

First, the text offers the timing of the vision from Daniel (8:1)

Daniel 8:1: In the third year of the reign of Belshazzar the king, a vision appeared to me, Daniel, subsequent to the one which appeared to me previously.

Daniel is careful to point out that this vision is an expansion of a previous one (chapter 7) given two years before. Belshazzar was the son of Nabonidus the King of Babylon, who ruled three years from that city before he left his throne to his son, while as he devoted himself to the worship of the moon god Sin in a desert oasis – a spiritual pilgrimage of sorts. Belshazzar became co-regent in 553 BCE, and was supposed to attend to Babylon's defense during his dad's journey. The year of the vision of chapter eight of Daniel either corresponds to the leaving of Nabonidus for his spiritual journey, and the ascension to sole ruler of Babylon by Belshazzar in about 550 BCE, or three years later (meaning the third year he was alone on the throne). By 540 BCE, Nabonidus returned when he heard the Persians planned to take the city of Babylon from his son by force. Nabonidus marched to face Cyrus the Mede, but was defeated and on October 10, 539 BCE, when he surrendered to Cyrus. Two days later the Persian armies overthrew the haughty city of Babylon that was engaged in a drunken party as Daniel recorded in our earlier lesson on Daniel 5. In any case, it is likely that Belshazzar was "flying solo" by the time of this vision.

Second, we are given the description of the vision by Daniel (8:2-14) along with the interpretation (which I have dropped in for simplicity sake from 8:15-24 after each part of the vision).

The record opens...*Daniel 8:2: I looked in the vision, and while I was looking, I was in the citadel of Susa, which is in the province of Elam; and I looked in the vision and I myself was beside the Ulai Canal.*

Apparently, Daniel was on a trip away from his normal dwelling, perhaps on some administrative duty. In any case, he was just living life, and God interrupted again – to help him see what the Most High was doing among men.

The vision he described had three main elements: A two-horned ram, a horned buck goat, and a specific horn that caught Daniel's attention. Right after explaining the three parts of the vision, Daniel shared HOW HE GOT THE INTERPRETATION, and then what each symbol meant. He wrote:

Daniel 8:15: When I, Daniel, had seen the vision, I sought to understand it; and behold, standing before me was one who looked like a man. 16 And I heard the voice of a man between [the banks of] Ulai, and he called out and said, "Gabriel, give this [man] an understanding of the vision." 17 So he came near to where I was standing, and when he came, I was frightened and fell on my face; but he said to me, "Son of man, understand that the vision pertains to the time of the end." 18 Now while he was talking with me, I sank into a deep sleep with my face to the ground; but he touched me and made me stand upright. 19 He said, "Behold, I am going to let you know what will occur at the final period of the indignation, for [it] pertains to the appointed time of the end.

This passage contained the first of the five passages in God's Word where the angel Gabriel was named. The next is found in Daniel 9, with all the remaining found in the first part of Luke's Gospel. Gabe explained that the vision wasn't about something happening right away – but rather it extended into the time of TRIBULATION, and the time of the END. That detail helps us recognize the prophecy had implications for a time yet in our future – so this won't simply be a "history lesson" for us.

In this lesson, we will add the interpretation to each part of the vision to make it clear and simple.

First, there was a ram with two horns: (8:3-4)

Daniel 8:3 Then I lifted my eyes and looked, and behold, a ram which had two horns was standing in front of the canal. Now the two horns [were] long, but one [was] longer than the other, with the longer one coming up last. 4 I saw the ram butting westward, northward, and southward, and no [other] beasts could stand before him nor was there anyone to rescue from his power, but he did as he pleased and magnified [himself].

- Two horns
- One higher than another
- Pushing in three directions
- Unstoppable greatness for a time

In the section on the interpretation, Daniel was told simply in *Daniel 8:20: The ram, which you saw with the two horns, represents the kings of Media and Persia.*

This means the vision was NOT going to contain any focus on the Babylonian kingdom as the previous visions in Daniel 2:19-45 and Daniel 7 had done. This vision began with the Medo-Persian Kingdom – matching the breast and arms of silver in Daniel 2, and the lop-sided bear of Daniel 7. Every time Daniel saw a vision with Medo-Persia, the heavenly view saw two uneven powers joined together. Here, it was one ram, but two uneven horns. The beginning of this kingdom was dominated by Media but fifty years later, the same kingdom was dominated by the Persians. The Medo-Persian Empire was vast and powerful, as the descriptions of Esther chapter one attest under Ahaseuras (or Xerxes). Yet, for all its power, as it drew nearer to its end, it kept facing a much smaller force of hoplite Greek armies, and **losing:**

- It started when the Athenians, with their democratic ideas, helped the Ionian cities of western Turkey revolt Persian king Darius I (550-486 BCE) and the Persian king swore to have revenge on Athens when he found them. He crushed the Ionians (494 BCE), putting down the revolt near Miletus, but needed to withdraw his army and not move on at that time against Athens to conquer a new people.

- Four years later, the Battle of Marathon was set in the end of August and beginning of September of 490 BCE, as Darius sent a naval task force across the Aegean, to take the Cycladic Islands and then attack Athens. Taking many islands, the Persians sailed for Athens, landing in nearby Marathon. Athenians marched to Marathon to meet the Persian advance and blocked the two exits from the plain of Marathon. After a five-day stalemate, the Athenian hoplites attacked the Persians, devastating the Persian infantry. The Persian force retreated to Asia, showing the Greeks that the Persians could be beaten. Although dubious, the legend of a Greek messenger Pheidippi'des running from Marathon to Athens with news of victory – a distance of just over 26 miles – and collapsing following the announcement, which became the inspiration for the so named athletic event introduced at the 1896 Athens Olympics.

- Darius began raising a huge new army with which to return to Greece, but faced an Egyptian uprising in 486 BCE. He died the same year in October of 486 BCE.

- His successor and son, Xerxes I (Ahaseurus of Esther) prepared a face saving second invasion of Greece. The preparations for that army were set at the party of Esther 1.

By 483 BCE, more than one-half of that year was spent on the massive and impressive party that staged the backdrop of the military planning sessions for the second invasion of Greece.

- In the summer heat of 480 BCE, the Greek city-states found themselves under attack again. Xerxes amassed a huge army and navy, and set out to conquer Greece and redeem his father's defeat. The Athenian general Themistocles proposed that the Greeks block the advance of the Persian army at the pass of Thermopylae, while blocking the Persian navy at the Straits of Artemisium.

- The Greek force of approximately 7,000 men thus marched north to block the pass in the summer of 480 BCE against a Persian army, alleged to have numbered over one million.

- Though vastly outnumbered, the Greeks knew the terrain and held off the Persians for three assaults over a weeklong period. King Leonidas I of Sparta blocked the only road by which the massive Persian army could pass. After the second day of battle, a local resident named Ephialtes betrayed the Greeks by revealing a small path that led behind the Greek lines. Aware that his force was being outflanked, Leonidas dismissed the bulk of the Greek army, and remained to guard the rear with 300 Spartans, 700 Thespians, 400 Thebans, and perhaps a few hundred others, the vast majority of whom were killed.

- After the defeat on land, the Greek navy at Artemisium evacuated Athens and withdrew to west of the island of Salamis, in the Saronic Gulf southwest of Athens. The Persians found an evacuated Athens, and followed the Greek ships – seeking decisive victory over them. The smaller and more maneuverable Greek fleet attacked the

Persian warships, and decimated them at the Battle of Salamis in late 480 BCE. Xerxes was forced to withdraw with much of his army to Asia Minor. The following year (August 479 BCE) the Persians were decisively defeated the Persians at the Battle of Plataea and Xerxes army returned home humbled.

- Since Esther was taken to Xerxes in December of 479 or January of 478 BCE according to Esther 2:16, the setting of Esther 2:1 and the "After these things" included the Greek wars and the news of the defeat of Xerxes army – along with the accompanying humiliation. The fought the inferior Greeks, and were defeated in the field. It was only a matter of time before the Greeks decided to fire back... and under a great leader, they eventually did about 150 years later in 333-323 BCE.

Second, there was a buck goat (8:5-8) that was to follow Medo-Persia – the Hellenic Kingdom of the Greeks.

Daniel 8:5 While I was observing, behold, a male goat was coming from the west over the surface of the whole earth without touching the ground; and the goat [had] a conspicuous horn between his eyes. 6 He came up to the ram that had the two horns, which I had seen standing in front of the canal, and rushed at him in his mighty wrath. 7 I saw him come beside the ram, and he was enraged at him; and he struck the ram and shattered his two horns, and the ram had no strength to withstand him. So he hurled him to the ground and trampled on him, and there was none to rescue the ram from his power. 8 Then the male goat magnified [himself] exceedingly. But as soon as he was mighty, the large horn was broken; and in its place there came up four conspicuous [horns] toward the four winds of Heaven.

- From the West
- Notable single horn
- Victory of the Buck Goat (8:7)
- Breaking of Great horn - rise of four horns (N,S,E,W)

In the section on the interpretation, Daniel was told simply in *Daniel 8:21: The shaggy goat [represents] the kingdom of Greece, and the large horn that is between his eyes is the first king. 22 "The broken [horn] and the four [horns that] arose in its place [represent] four kingdoms [which] will arise from [his] nation, although not with his power.*

God's revealed word here was no mystery – Greece would decisively destroy the Persian armies and take over when the time was right. Tracing the swift movement of Alexander the Great between 333-323 BCE is not difficult. Suffice it to say, that at the end of one decade on the road, Al had subdued Egypt, the Holy Land, Turkey, Iraq and Iran, and was standing on the edge of the Indus River having conquered more land in faster time than any army in the history of the world. Yet, the focus of the last part of the vision appeared to be dedicated to a specific vision of four rulers from within the kingdom that broke up the power base, and finally one specific ruler who rose with certain designs on God's people. That ruler became the third part of the vision…

Third, there was a little horn (8:9-15) that deserved specific attention.

Daniel 8:9 Out of one of them came forth a rather small horn, which grew exceedingly great toward the south, toward the east, and toward the Beautiful [Land]. 10 It grew up to the host of Heaven and caused some of the host and some of the stars to fall to the Earth, and it trampled them down. 11 It even magnified [itself] to be equal with the Commander of the host; and it removed the regular sacrifice from Him, and the place of His sanctuary was thrown down. 12 And on account of transgression the host will be given over [to the horn] along with the regular sacrifice; and it will fling truth to the ground and perform [its will] and prosper. 13 Then I heard a holy one speaking, and another holy one said to that particular one who was speaking, "How long will the vision [about] the regular sacrifice apply, while the transgression causes horror, so as to allow both the holy place and the host to be trampled?" 14 He said to me, "For 2,300 evenings [and] mornings; then the holy place will be properly restored."

I suspect that what we are looking at is actually a **dual description** –

- First of the Seleucid ruler Antiochus IV (cp. Daniel 11:21), and...
- A future ruler in the world that has not yet been revealed – but who will show himself during the time of the Great Tribulation, as indicated in a literal reading of Daniel 8:19.

If I am correct, we are reading about TWO MEN, each a type of the other.

- One came out of the four Diadoche Generals (Antiochus IV).
- He swept south and east and became great.
- He involved himself in the Holy Land's affairs.

Those traits applied to Antiochus – but there were more traits listed – and those appear to be something greater than the violations of the second century BCE ruler... they appear to be of another FUTURE ruler.

- That one caused some of the host and some of the stars to fall (8:10). This could be a reference to some type of air war in which Daniel saw firepower that was unfamiliar to him – but I suspect it was a foray into explaining the DEMONIC POWER behind his rise.

- He stopped sacrifices at the temple in Jerusalem and interrupted the lives of the observant Jewish people (8:11).

- Some of the host (army) of Heaven was given to him (8:12) – probably a reference to his command of forces in the unseen world as well as his political power.

- His term of office was determined by God (8:13-14). Measuring the time based on a 360-day calendar of ancient Jewry – this one was in office for between six and seven years – but well short of the seven. The idea may have been to communicate that he would not make it to the end of the seven years of Tribulation.

If the entire description we just read was meant to poetically describe Antiochus – that is fine. Some of it looks like more to me, but I cannot be sure. What is **clear** is that **by 8:23 Daniel's record appears to be pointing to a time much later than the ancient Greek ruler.** He wrote:

Daniel 8:23: In the latter period of their rule, when the transgressors have run [their course], a king will arise, insolent and skilled in intrigue. 24 His power will be mighty, but not by his [own] power, and he will destroy to an extraordinary degree and prosper and perform [his will]; he will destroy mighty men and the holy people. 25 And through his shrewdness he will cause deceit to succeed by his influence; and he will magnify [himself] in his heart, and he will destroy many while [they are] at ease. He will even oppose the Prince of princes, but he will be broken without human agency.

It is clear that the ruler is at a **later time period**. It is clear that he attains the office with some trickery and underhanded tactic. It is also clear that his remarkable power will be backed by more than meets the eye. He will do fierce damage –even to some who were well known to be powerful. He will harm the Jewish people. He will be self-aggrandizing and self-reliant. He will also be on a leash of life that God will pull back when the Father decides he is finished his damaging work.

Finally, we see the troubles of Daniel (8:26-27). Daniel found himself overwhelmed with the vision and near exhaustion needing inspiration and help.

Daniel 8:26: The vision of the evenings and mornings which has been told is true; but keep the vision secret, for [it] pertains to many days [in the future]. 27 Then I, Daniel, was exhausted and sick for days. Then I got up [again] and carried on the king's business; but I was astounded at the vision, and there was none to explain [it].

Daniel became distracted by the site of the march of pagans and immorality – and lost the ability to recognize what God was about to do through the darkness of men to bring His eventual and certain victory.

God answered a question Daniel held in his heart: "What is God going to do with His people if there are yet this many terrible pagan rulers and programs ahead?" Remember, the vision's record is in the Hebrew language, which may mean that it was not for "public consumption" of the pagans, but focused on God's dealings with His own people.

We must remember that a spiritual battle rages behind what we are seeing in the headlines, and God hasn't left the scene… He is weaving the tapestry of history to present His story to the cosmos. Even when politicians stab at God's moral standards and defame

God's people – God is working out the story. He hasn't lost control – **He is DOING SOMETHING**. We must also remember that **the story has a SINGLE WINNER**. In the end, God will settle all accounts. There is no power to match His. If you are standing with Him, you are already siding with the winner.

Enza was born into poverty, the product of an unknown father paying for minutes with her crack- using mother. She was born in a flophouse on an old mattress, and that would be some of the best of what she could expect from her early life. Unloved and unkempt, she struggled to gain basic nutrition and hygiene in her first years of life. Her mother was attentive one day, absent the next, guilty and weepy the third and on and on it went... Another young woman saw the struggling child and began to take a daily interest in seeing to it she was fed, clothed, and clean. Life was hard, but Enza grew, watched and learned. By the time she was eight, she learned to hide from her mother when men came to visit, because her mother would have sold away her body for another hit of a drug. Even before puberty, this young girl learned about life, exchanges, and controlling men. By the time she was an adult, she was jaded with a darkness that draws a curtain over hope and lived the life of a struggler and hustler – believing that life was all about negotiating away what you have to get what you want. Enza met Jesus the first time in the eyes and heart of Carl, a young man that offered her his sandwich because he said she looked hungry, but didn't ask for anything in return. This was a new experience in her adult life with men – kindness. Carl saw her a number of times, and always he smiled, helped, and was kind. He asked for nothing, and she concluded that he must not have wanted women – and left it at that. After a time, she asked him, "Why are you always nice to me?" He replied, "Well, two reasons. The first is because I like you. I think you are a really wonderful person!" Feeling a bit stupid about receiving a compliment, she interrupted, "What's the second reason?" He turned and looker her in the eye and said these simple words: "Because I have been where you are. I have lived through the hard life, and met a friend

Who rescued me." Carl shared Jesus with Enza, and she listened in half disbelief that One would come and die for her. Her disbelief wasn't so much about His loving character, but more about His sovereignty. "If there is a God like you say, where has He been in MY LIFE?" Carl smiled and said. "Bringing you to this bench, walking you to this minute, hurting for the abuses but knowing that today you would meet Him, and that would all change." Enza began to tear up. Could it be true? She found out that it was – because Carl showed it first, and spoke it second. (This is a real story: names and details changed for protection of the parties).

Stop for a moment. What would have happened if Carl had decided that God was simply unfair in HIS LIFE? What would have happened if HE focused on the injustices rather than on God's deliverance from his own rebellion? Carl would have become exactly what we become when we get angry and sickened by injustice of this world – he would have become ineffective as a witness.

He would have missed out on a new life, and Enza would have missed out on his effective witness. Carl knew what Daniel was learning…

The mature believer's view of the world should not be fixated on the temporary dominance of darkness, but rather on God at work – moving history toward His purposes.

Shine the Light
Lessons in Daniel

Lesson Ten: Daniel 9:1-24 "Off the Bench" (Part One)

I have to admit that one of my favorite things to do is watch someone who is excellent in their craft do their work. I am that guy who ends up standing there for an hour to watch a person make art out of blown glass in a mall. I have come to realize that someone is truly great at their work when they make something that is very difficult look simple. That's why I love to watch Yo Yo Ma play a cello, because the instrument seems like an extension of his personality! Have you ever stopped to watch two world-class ice skaters on television move around a skating arena and perform their fluid motions that would leave you in traction if you tried them? Unless you are very unusual, you never thought to yourself, "You know, I could do that if I had a good pair of skates!" You looked with awe and real respect at what these fine athletes were able to complete after literally thousands of hours of practice. To do something well, it often takes enormous effort. If you get really good at it, it won't look like it took much effort at all.

The truth is that no one got to the level of success in his craft without regularly practicing some disciplines of mind and body. People spend hours learning techniques, all in anticipation of finding reward in doing what they do well. I think we all accept that most successful musicians practice long hours and even that athletes that compete spend vast periods of time in practice. Yet, there is a group that has captured my attention that also has had to study, practice, and hone their craft that you may never have thought of – servants. If you have ever been in a fine dining establishment, or on a five-star cruise ship, you have seen them at work. It takes much more than a stiff costume and a white pair of gloves to be a fine servant or steward. It's funny how we KNOW things take work, but we somehow think servants just KNOW what we need and how to get it in front of us. The fact is that even good table service requires excellent training.

While it is true that few of us harbor within the hopes of becoming world class athletes, excellent and highly paid cellists, or even "food server to the stars" – we DO have a goal to become great servants of God. We have been given some excellent examples as instructors… and the prophet Daniel from ancient Babylon was certainly among the best for both LIVING with and for God as well as LEAVING BEHIND an example to follow. His life revealed two secrets to becoming a strong and loving follower of God: the secret discipline of daily connection and the secret to joyful living in God's promises. By reading his journal, it will become clear….

Admittedly, Daniel can be quite confusing.

First, it is not organized in chronological order. For those of us who like linear organization, we wish the book followed IN ORDER the four kings in the book and their chapters. Technically the first and the last of the list are kings, and the two middle rulers were regents or governors appointed by an absent king. If you place all four in their order, the book would look more like this:

Nebuchadnezzar – King of Babylon (602-562 BCE).

Nebuchadnezzar was the king of the Neo-Babylonian Empire that defeated the rival armies to his west in the spring and summer of the year 605 at the battle of Carchemish. He was the king in whose name Daniel and his three friends Hananiah, Mishael and Azariah were brought to Babylon later that year. Under his reign, the first four chapters of Daniel reveal stories like the flourishing of the kosher kids in Daniel 1, the vision of the big statue in Daniel 2, the "fiery furnace" set up against Daniel's three companions in Daniel 3 and the vision of the tree in Daniel 4. That last vision set Nebuchadnezzar in a field for a period of time, prophesying that he would lose his mind and then have it restored when he humbled himself before God. You get the impression in the first four chapters that the theme of the time under Nebuchadnezzar was "God wants you to know Him, O king!"

After Nebuchadnezzar, the record of Daniel skips a number of rulers. Several men in the family competed for throne after the great king's death, including his son Evil-Merodach, who ruled for two years (562-560 BCE). He was murdered by Nebuchadnezzar's son-in-law Neriglissar (Nergal Sharezar). He, in turn, only lasted four years from 560-556 BCE and died. His son, Labasi-Marduk, replaced him for two short months in 556 BCE and was assassinated by Nabonidus, father of Belshazzar, who became a longer reigning king. After three years, he installed his son in office and left for a spiritual pilgrimage. The story in Daniel picks up after Belshazzar has been seated in the throne as a regent for his dad.

Belshazzar – co-regent of Babylon (553-539 BCE)

Belshazzar was a grandson of Nebuchadnezzar by one of the great king's daughters. He wasn't near the top of the list of rulers, but the others all got "bumped off" by relatives, and he and his dad rose in the line each time. Nabonidus was king, but Daniel seldom saw him, because Daniel stayed in Babylon with his son to advise him during the dad's pilgrimage years. It was during that time that three important prophetic stories unfolded:

Chapter 7 – Four Beasts, Little Horn, Ancient of Days, 553 BCE – 1st year of Belshazzar. Like the four kingdoms shared with Nebuchadnezzar years before, God wanted the Gentile regent of the world's largest empire to know about the progression of kings yet to come.

Chapter 8 – Ram and the Buck Goat, 551 BCE – 3rd year of Belshazzar. God was intent that Daniel would have even more insight into the political and prophetic coming of Medo-Persian kings, because he would live to see them rule. Further, he would see all the way through to their end and the rise of Greece under Alexander and the four generals (Diadoche) that would eventually replace him.

Chapter 5 – Writing on the Wall, 539 BCE – the night Belshazzar died. Nabonidus was outside Babylon defeated by Cyrus the Mede, as the kingdom that would replace Babylon was about to take the city. Inside the city, Belshazzar was hosting a great feast when God interrupted and let him know that his days of rule were over by writing on a wall with His own hand.

Darius – Governor of Babylon under Cyrus (559-530 BCE)

Cyrus took over the city of Babylon on the death of Belshazzar and conquered the city, replacing the Great Babylonian Empire with that of the Empire of the Medes and Persians. Essentially, Iraq was overrun by Iran (if you want to think of it in oversimplified modern country terms). When Cyrus became king, there was still much to do to secure the satrapies of the Babylonian kingdom, so he appointed a governor and journeyed off for a time. He placed in Babylon a trusted companion named Darius as governor and proclaimed him a "king" over that part of the larger empire. It is during his "reign" that God spoke dramatically about the coming days of kings and kingdoms in three stories:

Chapter 9 – Seventy Weeks, circa 539 BCE – 1st year of Darius.

Daniel saw the time drawing near the captivity of the Jewish people should have been ending, and he became anxious, as he saw little movement to end their plight. He sought God, and Gabriel was dispatched to tell him what was going to happen all the way to the Kingdom of Righteousness – at the time of the very end.

Chapters 11-12 – Coming Conflicts North and South, 539 BCE – 1st year of Darius.

With even greater detail concerning the Jewish people and their subjection under Hellenistic powers from Greece, God detailed to Daniel the plight of the Jews under western domination until the end times.

Chapter 6 – Lion's Den, c.538-534 BCE under Darius, not dated.

At some point in Daniel's tenure as an older counselor, he got other counselors upset. It was likely early in Darius' "reign," because the advisors were able to trick him into signing a decree that eventually backfired, but the "Lion's Den" story of Daniel is set under Darius as well.

Cyrus – King of Persia (550-530 BCE)

Cyrus had been on the throne since he took Babylon from Belshazzar, but in Chapter 10 – The "Vision of Delayed Angelic Help" – 536 BCE – 3rd year of Cyrus – all the visions of the period were ascribed to the time of the governor Darius. In chapter 10, it doesn't mention Darius, but dates the message between God and Daniel to the third year of Cyrus, or 536 BCE. This is the last of the visions of the book that is given, and can rightly be placed under

Darius as well because he was governor – yet he is not mentioned.

The book dances around the timeline to organize the materials under THEMES instead of keeping a strict timeline. Add to that the fact that the writer uses the term "king" loosely, since that is the way he referred to the men on the throne in person, and the whole of the twelve chapters can seem jumbled.

Second, the book can be confusing. The book is laced with wild scenes that were prophecies of coming kingdoms. The major components of those scenes were difficult and are often interpreted inside the narrative with words like: "The beasts that you saw were kingdoms." That isn't the tough part. The difficulty comes when you are trying to understand the specifics of what we are to learn about these kingdoms, based solely on these descriptions. Commentators don't have problems with the general frame, but seem to find the details difficult to nail down with certainty. Some people have a terrible time when not EVERYTHING lines up clearly for them, and they "shut down" because they "don't get it."

A third and final reason Daniel's writing can be confusing is this: The prophesies are accompanied by highlights of how Daniel and his friends were able to be a reliable witness for all four using disciplines of walk – and these can be easily obscured by all the fantastic details of each prophecy. It is easy to think there are SERIOUS SECTIONS of the book – like prophetic utterances of future days – that belong to the ADULT BIBLE FELLOWSHIP, while the other parts of the book are just cute little stories for the CHILDREN'S DEPARTMENT.

Sometimes we miss the connection between the PROPHECIES and the VESSELS God used to speak His Word. This is what I want to focus on in this lesson. We want to drop into the scene of

Daniel's personal Bible study and prayer life that became the setting of the exciting promises God made known to him.

Let me be clear: the disciplines of Daniel gave rise to the blessings and insights of Daniel – and they will to you as well. God will speak into your life with clarity when you learn to surrender that life to Him.

Don't be afraid that applying the word "discipline" to your walk with God will make you a Pharisee. In the loose living Christianity of our day, some of us have wrongly come to see GRACE as a "get out of Hell free card," and any words that sound like we must work at our relationship with God sound like a "work's based salvation." That isn't what I am talking about at all.

I am simply saying that godliness is never accidental.

A relationship with God comes by God's favor through seeing His Word as truth – as God reaches into our lives and energizes a new life within. Yet, following God is marked by surrender to His Word resulting in becoming more like the character of our Savior. That comes by adopting specific disciplines of heart, mind and body.

Jesus didn't preach against disciplines – He spoke against being a "show off" in your walk with God. It wasn't PRAYER that Jesus was speaking against, but loud trumpets blasting the prayer of the Pharisee in the streets. It wasn't RIGHTEOUSNESS Jesus was against, it was the display "to be seen of men" that He abhorred.
Let me drive the truth of Daniel 9 home once more, and then we will walk through five key character traits that showed through in Daniel's life...

Key Principle: At the heart of our walk with God, there are DISCIPLINES of our walk and PROMISES of our God. Living in BOTH will help us to walk boldly and with strength through times of trouble.

Daniel 9 offers **five character traits** that God honored and highlighted in Daniel:

The first "discipline" or "character trait" was what I will simply call PERCEPTION:

The whole revelation of the truth of the end times came to Daniel when the man took God's Word seriously, studied it thoroughly, and believed it literally.

When a believer forms his life and perceives truth based on God's Word – that is the life of FAITH. Look at the first two verses of Daniel 9, because they reveal both the TIMING of the revelation, and the TENSION that brought the revelation about:

Daniel 9:1 In the first year of Darius the son of Ahasuerus of Median descent, who was made king over the kingdom of the Chaldeans 2 in the first year of his reign, I, Daniel, observed in the books the number of the years which was [revealed as] the word of the LORD to Jeremiah the prophet for the completion of the desolations of Jerusalem, [namely], seventy years.

This is a great passage. A man of God is reading the Word of God and takes it seriously, but cannot relate the apparent promise of the passage to what he sees around him. He was reading places like *Jeremiah 29:10, For thus says the LORD, 'When seventy years have been completed for Babylon, I will visit you and fulfill My good word to you, to bring you back to this place."* The problem is that that was said at the BEGINNING of the binding of the Gentiles which was about sixty-seven years before. Did Daniel misunderstand what Jeremiah said? After all, the FINAL AND COMPLETE CAPTIVITY didn't occur until Zedekiah's children were slaughtered and his eyes were put out, and that was twenty years later. Was THAT date the beginning of the clock? Daniel didn't know. He THOUGHT the return was coming soon, and he was getting nervous when the authorities around him didn't seem to be signaling that return.

Don't skip over the fact that Daniel answered what appeared to be POLITICAL issues with prayer and the study of the Word of God. The simple fact is that Daniel was more concerned with the words of Jeremiah the Prophet than the words of the Babylonian Daily Chronicle. Is that true of us? Do we spend more energy in extracting truth from Scripture that in trying to figure out truth from the editorially laden news shows of our day?

I think one of the blessings of the record Daniel Nine was that the prophet was simply concerned with a promise of seventy years of captivity, when Gabriel made it clear the real issue would not be resolved for seventy blocks of seven years!

It occurs to me that we tend to see things in much smaller ways than God wants to show to us. We don't think in ions, but in election cycles. God is working the whole plan – and we would be unwise to think that we can truly gain much understanding of our times up close. It may take one thousand years to see how what is happening in our world today will be resolved by the Prince of Peace.

Let me dig further... We need to handle even our own life history with humility. You may have met the most important person in God's plan for you in a waiting room on a Tuesday afternoon. You may share Jesus with someone at a bus stop that will lead to a national change and an international revival. We think too small and see too little to really grasp what God is doing in and through us.

Daniel had the PERCEPTION that truth comes from God's Word, and that is where he invested his energy. It paid off – it always does.

The second "discipline" or "character trait" that we see in Daniel was a FOCUSED PURPOSE:

Look very closely at the passage and you can pick out where Daniel sought peace and clarity. It wasn't simply from the Word – though that set the stage as we said already... The clarity came, not simply by study of the Word- but by deeply emotional, extensive times of seeking God. Daniel didn't just seek ANSWERS, he SOUGHT GOD.

Daniel 10:3 So I gave my attention to the Lord God to seek [Him by] prayer and supplications, with fasting, sackcloth and ashes. 4 I prayed to the LORD my God and confessed and said...

- One who seeks answers from the past is an historian.
- One who seeks answers from humanity and culture is an anthropologist.
- One who seeks answers from a *Bible* is a theologian.
- One who seeks answers from God is a believer…

Don't think I am suggesting the other disciplines are unnecessary or optional for a complete understanding of truth – that is NOT what I am saying. I am repeating the words of Jesus. He said: *"You search the Scriptures because you think that in them you have eternal life; it is these that testify about Me." (John 5:39).* The answer isn't found simply by UNDERSTANDING THE TEXT. **The answers are found by**

SEEKING THE LORD. Daniel knew this, and sought God with prayer and humble confession.

I think it is a bit humorous and encouraging that God's answering messenger came almost as a startling interruption – because He was seeking to settle in God's arms, not get an answer to every question! Gabriel showed up, and it was the record of one of those moments like when Peter came to the door of a prayer meeting praying for his release from prison and was left standing outside in Acts 12. It seems that often God's answer takes us completely off guard, even though we have been deliberately ASKING HIM A QUESTION. Why am I still surprised after all these years of following God that He still answers us? He doesn't always do it right away, but when He does, I must remember to take time to celebrate His answers – and not simply move on in my list of needs and questions…

John Owen, a Puritan writer, wrote: What an individual is in secret on his knees before God, that's who he really is, and no more.

Daniel's FOCUS wasn't simply on the problem of the seventy years coming ton end, but on KNOING GOD better – and that became his life purpose.

When he sought to know God – the Lord answered him by meeting the other needs of his life. As Jesus said (recorded in *Mt. 6:33): Seek first the Kingdom of God and His righteousness, and all these things will be added to you.*

Just remember that FOCUS on God is most hindered by FOCUS ON SELF. Pride kills godliness.

The story is told of two ducks and a frog that lived happily together in a farm pond. They were great friends and enjoyed playing together. When the hot days of summer came, however, the pond began to dry up. They soon realized that they had to move. This was no problem for the ducks because they could just fly to another pond, but the frog was stuck. So they decided to put a stick in the bill of each duck that the frog could hang onto with his mouth as they flew to another pond. The plan worked well - so well, in fact, that as they were flying along a farmer looked up in admiration and said, "Well, isn't that a clever idea! I wonder who thought of that?" To which the frog said, "I did..." Be careful of pride - it can cause you to fall!

The third "discipline" or "character trait" that Daniel exhibited was PERSONALIZATION:

Daniel's prayers didn't DISTANCE him from the responsibility of his situation, but drew him INTO the situation as one who personally felt the pain.

God won't reveal Himself to the armchair theologian and theoretical philosopher – He isn't content with someone who is curious about truth. He comes to the HUNGRY and NEEDY of heart.

Look carefully at the prayer of Daniel to uncover his heart:

Daniel 9:4b Alas, O Lord, the great and awesome God, who keeps His covenant and loving kindness for those who love Him and keep His commandments, 5 we have sinned, committed iniquity, acted wickedly and rebelled, even turning aside from Your commandments and ordinances. 6 Moreover, we have not listened to Your servants the prophets, who spoke in Your name to our kings, our princes, our fathers and all the people of the land. 7 Righteousness belongs to You, O Lord, but to us open shame, as it is this day– to the men of Judah, the inhabitants of Jerusalem and all Israel, those who are nearby and those who are far away in all the countries to which You have driven them, because of their unfaithful deeds which they have committed against

You. 8 Open shame belongs to us, O Lord, to our kings, our princes and our fathers, because we have sinned against You. 9 To the Lord our God [belong] compassion and forgiveness, for we have rebelled against Him; 10 nor have we obeyed the voice of the LORD our God, to walk in His teachings which He set before us through His servants the prophets. 11 Indeed all Israel has transgressed Your law and turned aside, not obeying Your voice; so the curse has been poured out on us, along with the oath which is written in the law of Moses the servant of God, for we have sinned against Him. 12 Thus He has confirmed His words which He had spoken against us and against our rulers who ruled us, to bring on us great calamity; for under the whole heaven there has not been done [anything] like what was done to Jerusalem. 13 As it is written in the Law of Moses, all this calamity has come on us; yet we have not sought the favor of the LORD our God by turning from our iniquity and giving attention to Your truth. 14 Therefore the LORD has kept the calamity in store and brought it on us; for the LORD our God is righteous with respect to all His deeds which He has done, but we have not obeyed His voice. 15 And now, O Lord our God, Who have brought Your people out of the land of Egypt with a mighty hand and have made a name for Yourself, as it is this day– we have sinned, we have been wicked. 16 O Lord, in accordance with all Your righteous acts, let now Your anger and Your wrath turn away from Your city Jerusalem, Your holy mountain; for because of our sins and the iniquities of our fathers, Jerusalem and Your people [have become] a reproach to all those around us. 17 So now, our God, listen to the prayer of Your servant and to his supplications, and for Your sake, O Lord, let Your face shine on Your desolate sanctuary. 18 O my God, incline Your ear and hear! Open Your eyes and see our desolations and the city which is called by Your name; for we are not presenting our supplications before You on account of any merits of our own, but on account of Your great compassion. 19 O Lord, hear! O Lord, forgive! O Lord, listen and take action! For Your own sake, O my God, do not delay, because Your city and Your people are called by Your name.

Notice first the simplicity of the prayer:

- It began with a focus on the person and power of God – together with His faithful character (9:4).

- It clearly acknowledged responsibility of sin on him and his people and not on God's poor oversight (9:5-10).

- It showed that he understood the captivity to be according to God's Words (9:11-14).

- It recognized God's past goodness and rescue (9:15-16).

- It made clear Daniel's request to see the seventy years finished soon (9:17-19).

You cannot help but be struck with a sense that **Daniel felt attached to his people and responsible for their sin.**

There is no hint of distance and individualism that would separate him from the fallen and broken people of the Jews.

Someone has written: We are much better at making excuses than confessing sin. We live in a "no-fault" culture where you can get "no-fault" insurance, and a "no-fault" divorce. The mantra of our modern culture is, "Hey, it's not my fault." And we've come up with some pretty names to excuse our sin. We say, "I goofed" or "I blew it" or we talk about "mistakes" or "weaknesses." What we call an "affair," God calls "adultery." What we call "a little weakness," God calls "wickedness." What we call "a mistake," God calls "madness." Proverbs 28:13 says, *"He who conceals his sins does not prosper, but whoever confesses and renounces them finds mercy."*

In our day, we're quick to point out other peoples' mistakes, but we have a hard time admitting when we've blown it. Here are some actual excerpts from insurance companies where individuals who had accidents explained what went wrong:

- Coming home, I drove into the wrong house and collided with a tree that I don't own.
- The other guy was all over the road and I had to swerve a number of times before I hit him.
- I had been driving my car for 40 years when I fell asleep at the wheel and had an accident.
- The telephone pole approached my car at a rapid speed, as I swerved to get out of its way, it hit me.
- I pulled away from the side of the road, glanced at my mother-in-law, and drove over the embankment.

Daniel PERSONALIZED the troubles and repented. He placed himself with the sinners and not with the righteous "APART." He knew that God would give grace to the humble and he was convinced he had no reason to think he was better than others were.

The fourth "discipline" or "character trait" was what I will call ATTENTIVENESS:

God poured out far more than Daniel asked – and that was totally unexpected by Daniel. God did the unexpected – because He can. Yet the end of verse 23 may offer the key as to why God offered such a broad and complete word to Daniel:

Daniel 9:22 He gave [me] instruction and talked with me and said, "O Daniel, I have now come forth to give you insight with understanding. 23 At the beginning of your supplications the command was issued, and I have come to tell [you], for you are highly esteemed; so give heed to the message and gain understanding of the vision."

Jesus said that only the disciple who "takes heed" to His words will truly benefit by them. Near the close of the "Sermon on the Mount" in Matthew 7 Jesus made the point:

24 Therefore everyone who hears these words of Mine and acts on them, may be compared to a wise man who built his house on the rock. 25 And the rain fell, and the floods came, and the winds blew and slammed against that house; and [yet] it did not fall, for it had been founded on the rock. 26 Everyone who hears some words of Mine and does not act on them will be like a foolish man who built his house on the sand. 27 The rain fell, and the floods came, and the winds blew and slammed against that house; and it fell– and great was its fall.

It is not BEING IN THE VICINITY of the teaching of God's Word that will help you, but heeding what you hear from God's Word. Don't be too proud to listen to truth when God delivers it.

D.L. Moody put it this way: Be humble or you'll stumble.

The issue isn't whether you MEMORIZED the Word, but if you FOLLOW the Word. It isn't, "Do you attend church often?" but rather, "Do you listen and change because of what God's Word says?" Jesus made it clear – storms come in life to both those who heed His Word and those who don't – but only those who HEED have the foundation to stand.

Daniel practiced ATTENTIVENESS to God's Word, and that made him a trustworthy target for God to open his eyes to the deepest of truths.

The final "discipline" or "character trait" exhibited by Daniel was PATIENCE.

Though God offered an answer right away, but wasn't going to bring those truths about for generations. He is a PROCESS God. In the meantime, a believer was called to continue to live in the joy of the promises, trusting in His Word.

Daniel 9:20 Now while I was speaking and praying, and confessing my sin and the sin of my people Israel, and presenting my supplication before the LORD my God in behalf of the holy mountain of my God, 21 while I was still speaking in prayer, then the man Gabriel, whom I had seen in the vision previously, came to me in [my] extreme weariness about the time of the evening offering. 24 "Seventy weeks have been decreed for your people and your holy city, to finish the transgression, to make an end of sin, to make atonement for iniquity, to bring in everlasting righteousness, to seal up vision and prophecy and to anoint the most holy [place]..."

Some are waiting for me to unravel the "seventy weeks" prophecy, and **our next lesson will seek to do that** – but first, there is a timely question we must answer…

ARE YOU READY? Are you ready for God to open up to you what He is doing now and in the future? **Can He trust US** with a message of PROMISES because they will carefully be handled by followers who walk in the DISCIPLINES of a believer?

Daniel knew that God understood what he could not, and he was content with God running the world. **Are YOU?**

Be very careful never to get to the place in your walk where you believe God OWES you an explanation for doing things in a different way than you think they ought to be done! Follow Jesus. Love Him sincerely. Put on the disciplines of a believer. Why? Because…At the heart of our walk with God,

there are DISCIPLINES of our walk to be practiced and PROMISES from our God to be trusted.

Living in BOTH will help us to walk boldly and with strength through times of trouble.

Shine the Light
Lessons in Daniel

Lesson Eleven: Daniel 9-12 "Peering into the Darkness"

I don't like caves, and I have never been partial to bats... in fact they really creep me out. During my archaeological training, a group of young students in Jerusalem – my roommates and I – decided to go exploring in some caves in Wadi Tekoa, a site in the Judean Wilderness near the ancient home of the Prophet Amos. The caves were not excavated, and still retained all their antiquities, most of which were buried as much as twenty feet below the surface of the current cave floor. What I didn't know at the time was that much the floor was nothing more than bat dung... several feet of bat dung... old bat dung from hundreds of years of bat relief! The word "disgusting doesn't 'scratch the surface' – if you will forgive the obvious pun!

Worse than the condition of the floor were the residents on the ceiling, lined with an innumerable scene of winged, hanging, hairy rodents. The bats were thick in the cave, and the cave was as dark as pitch, even though outside the cave, it was midday and the burning desert sun was relentless. The only thing about the cave experience that was pleasant was the cool air... a very slight breeze that eased out of the cave from deep inside the darkness. What I found most unsettling was that I could not see as we crawled forward. If we used a flashlight, it stirred the bats and they would pelt our lights and us. If we didn't – there was only a very eerie darkness, and no way to perceive the depth of the cave or where we were in relationship to the opening... it was a scary experience I will do my best never to repeat. I have come to realize that I treasure my sight. I love color and visual beauty. I can sit in a gallery, look at a famous Monet for an hour, and not realize the time was passing... I hate the thought of not being able to see. My cave experience cemented that fear within...

What is true of physical sight is also true in most of us when we think of the future. We cannot really see where the story that God is designing is headed on our own. Our nation has made such dramatic changes in our lifetime; most of us confess we cannot begin to reckon the course of the coming years. We simply cannot peer into the darkness... but we who know God know a secret – there is nothing too dark for His eye. He can see it all. He is weaving the tapestry of history, and He knows where it goes and what story it will reveal when all the threads are in place. Sometimes He decides to share it with a believer, and even better, lets that follower share it with us. The prophecies of an ancient Jew in captivity in Babylon are a record of just those very truths – God shining a light forward in the dark cave of the future of His people...

Key Principle: History is "His" story – and God is never surprised by it. The path of the future is as the path of the past in His eye – secure, known and unwavering from the Master Craftsman's hand.

Today we glimpse directly into the cave, in a set of prophecies given hundreds of years before Christ, that all but spell out His name before He was born. That peering ahead includes much detail that to Daniel was prophecy, but to us it is history. To God, the past and the future are the same – finished in His mind.... Let's look at the course of the future of the Jewish people as exposed from the shrouded darkness to Daniel.

There are seven parts recorded in the book to the prophecies Daniel received during the first year of Darius the Mede.

Unfortunately, they have been divided into separated chapters in Daniel 9, and then rejoined in Daniel 11 and 12. We will look at the whole picture together, though we cannot tell if Daniel received the whole picture at one time, or over the course of that first year.

Part One: The "big frame" of the future of God's chosen people was offered. This vision included an over view from rebuilding Jerusalem, Messiah's coming and departure, and a Period of Great Tribulation (9:24-27).

Part Two: Starting "now:" the immediate future of the Media Kingdom (11:1) **was revealed to encourage the Persian ruler.**

Part Three: "Buck Goat" rising: the coming rise of the Hellenic Kingdom (Alexander and the Diadoche – 11:2-4) was predicted.

Part Four: Divisions and Strife: the battles of Hellenic Monarchies (Seleucids and Ptolemies) are revealed (11:5-20).

Part Five: Template: a Seleucid ruler shows the pattern of hatred toward God's people (Antiochus IV – 11:21-36).

Part Six: Destroyer: a future ruler = the hateful Antichrist was described (Daniel 11:36-45).

Part Seven: Free at Last: the restoration of the Jewish people was made clear (Daniel 12).

Of this detailed list, we will choose two prophecies to look at with greater intensity – because they are the ones most relevant to the present and future story of God's move through and in His people... We will examine "Part One" and "Part Six" – the vision of the coming Christ (9:24-27) and the vision of the coming Anti-Christ (11:36-45) with only a quick nod to the stories of the other prophecies.

Look closely at **Part One**, and watch the entrance and exit of Messiah...

Part One: The "big frame" of the future of God's chosen people was offered.

This vision included an over view from rebuilding Jerusalem, Messiah's coming and departure, and a Period of Great Tribulation (9:24-27).

Daniel 9:24 Seventy weeks have been decreed for your people and your holy city, to finish the transgression, to make an end of sin, to make atonement for iniquity, to bring in everlasting righteousness, to seal up vision and prophecy and to anoint the most holy place. 25 So you are to know and discern that from the issuing of a decree to restore and rebuild Jerusalem until Messiah the Prince there will be seven weeks and sixty- two weeks; it will be built again, with plaza and moat, even in times of distress. 26 Then after the sixty- two weeks the Messiah will be cut off and have nothing, and the people of the prince who is to come will destroy the city and the sanctuary. And its end will come with a flood; even to the end, there will be war; desolations are determined. 27 And he will make a firm covenant with the many for one week, but in the middle of the week he will put a stop to sacrifice and grain offering; and on the wing of abominations will come one who makes desolate, even until a complete destruction, one that is decreed, is poured out on the one who makes desolate.

Look closely as this incredibly detailed prophecy was disclosed:
Remember it came through desperate prayer (9:20-21) by a prophet that was holding God to a literal fulfillment of His Word. It was delivered by an angelic messenger (9:22-23). He opened a "decree" from Heaven (9:24-27), and it was about a period of time – some "Seventy Weeks." The description is VERY SPECIFIC:

- The full-extended time was decreed specifically for the Jewish people and Jerusalem (9:24a). God placed a limit on how long everything in their future would continue and closed the plan's end.

- The end of the time would leave a fully atoned Jewish people, a permanent disposal of all their unrighteousness, an end to all prophecy, and a pure place of worship in the holiest place of the Temple (9:24b). This was not a mere statement that the atonement would be PROVIDED, but rather that the atonement would be EFFECTIVE. Interpreters that reckon this to be a reference to the COMING of Messiah, fail to grasp this prophecy is not only about the availability of the ultimate solution to sin – but the actual resolution of the disobedient people and their defiled worship center!

- The announced time clock commenced with the human decree to restore and rebuild Jerusalem – which could have been one of four such times Jerusalem was "restarted" (9:25):

    1. Cyrus II and the original decree (538/537 BCE)
    2. Darius or Cyaxeres (c. 519 BCE)
    3. Artaxerxes to Ezra (c 458 BCE)
    4. Artaxerxes to Nehemiah (445 BCE, Neh. 1)

The last one appears to be the correct one – because it fits the whole of the narrative's detail. This is the only decree that is explicit to include the defenses of the city. The walls and gates were still broken down when this decree was given. This decree was given in March of 445 BCE (cp. Neh. 2:1-8). If that is correct, the clock started at that point, and explains the essential nature of why God provided the record of Nehemiah (beyond the fact that it is a great story!).

- The unfolding of time is told in SABBATICAL YEARS—in groups of seven years – just as the people had neglected the celebration of those over a long period of 490 years and now were in captivity for seventy years to correct this specific desecration of the land. *2 Chron. 36:21* says, *The land enjoyed its Sabbath rests; all the time of its desolation it rested, until the seventy years were completed in fulfillment of the word of the LORD spoken by Jeremiah"* (a reference to Jeremiah 25:11). After 69 blocks of seven years (9:25), Messiah the Prince would come. That left us with a MATH PROBLEM if the sixty-nine sevens were consecutive and unbroken – which was not certain in the prophecy. In that case, commencing with decree to restore Jerusalem (plaza and moat) until Messiah the Prince comes was to be 69 x 7, reckoned as 483 years. If we count the time between the decree given in March of 445 BCE (cp. Neh. 2:1-8) in 69 sets of Sabbatical years (seven year blocks), using the 360 day year common to the time, we move forward 173,880 days, ending on or about 32-33 CE with Messiah the Prince. That appears to be in the reference of Jesus' announcement in Luke 19 at Palm Sunday.

To be clear, I didn't discover this problem. It was long ago documented by Sir Robert Anderson, who developed the chronology based on March 14, 445 BCE. That date was later corrected by scholars as 444 BCE. The dates of the end of this period have also been carefully studied and debated, as there are a few variables – leap years, the year "0" etc, and the point is that it brings all scholars to a date between 30 CE and 33 CE – the time of Jesus' appearance in Jerusalem.

- After Messiah entered the scene, according to the prophecy, He will be somehow reduced to "having nothing" in the wake of a Wicked Prince and his people that will destroy the Temple and the City. This appears to be a reference to the Crucifixion, followed by the destruction of the upper city of Jerusalem and her temple that occurred in 70 CE (9:26).

- A sustained period that includes unending wars and desolations in the region of the Near East (9:26) is detailed, until a political entity appears that can settle the strife with a pleasing treaty that appears to uphold all parties for a period of time (9:27a). The key player in making this treaty will also be the one who violates it after three and one half years (9:27b) as war revives. By the end of that conflict, the treaty maker (and breacher) is slain (9:27b).

The overall frame, then, was this:

1. Decree and Return from Babylon
2. Coming of Messiah
3. Cutting off of Messiah
4. Destruction of Jerusalem
5. Near East Wars and Strife
6. An Eventual Peace Treaty
7. The Violation of the Treaty by its Creator
8. A Time of Destruction and Warfare
9. The Death of the Violator

Wow, that is clear! **Can we prove that Daniel was written as predictive prophecy BEFORE the events it detailed?** Sure, we can!

Cave four of the eleven caves found near Qumran (of the so-called "Dead Sea Scrolls"), seems to indicate that Daniel was a treasured by that community – because so many fragments of that work were found. The "Yahad" community of Qumran lived during a very anxious period and may have thought the end prophecies were being fulfilled in their day.

Though it is true that the fragments of 4QDanc, published in November 1989, do not include but a few words from Daniel 9 (scraps from Cave 4 contain "five tiny fragments, all from the prayer in chapter 9 but none with more than one complete word"), and 12 – these have not been discerned from the fragments as yet – the rest of the writing was dated to the C2 BCE. This allowed us to demonstrate chapter 11 comments of the Hellenistic period of wars as clear, detailed, predictive prophecy! This also forces the date of the original writing back before that time, as copies were clearly being made by the C2 BCE for distribution of a document that internally dates itself to the C6 BCE.

(*The most extensively preserved scroll of the book of Daniel from Qumran is 4QDana, which contains large portions of Daniel. Preserved are parts of Daniel 1:16–20; 2:9–11, 19–49; 3:1, 2; 4:29, 30; 5:5–7, 12–14, 16–19; 7:5–7, 25–28; 8:1–5; 10:16–20; 11:13–16. Scroll 4QDanb contains Daniel 5:10–12, 14–16, 19–22; 6:8–22, 27–29; 7:1–6, 11(?), 26–28; 8:1–8, 13–16; and 4QDanc has Daniel 10:5–9, 11–16, 21; 11:1, 2, 13–17, 25–29 (Ulrich 1987:18.)*

The lesson here is unmistakable. **God isn't "making up the plan" in response to men's ideas and strategies, nor is He flexing based on the work of His enemy**.

- God has the plan – and God is working it.
- Men can reject God's right to do so – but that won't change anything.
- The enemy can lie and tell us that God has lost control – but that doesn't make it so.
- When God set the plan of human history in place that was the plan.

When Job asked God about WHY terrible things happened, God answered without any sense of defensiveness and merely replied:

Job 38:2 Who is this that darkens counsel by words without knowledge?

That doesn't seem like much of an answer – but the very question implies something that is NOT at all true – that we have the standing to question the Creator. I am not His peer, nor am I able to think on His level. **That is the simple fact, regardless of how I feel about it. Professional ball players don't need tips from amateurs, nor do they truly benefit from the shouted insights of angry fans.** The Creator the immediate future of the Media isn't a Heavenly parent that is desperate to make me happy at the expense of the truth. It may sound harsh, but when I express an arrogant attitude of equality – truth is the right prescription to set me straight.

Part Two: Starting "now:" the immediate future of the Media Kingdom (11:1 was revealed to encourage the Persian ruler.)

God not only opened the door to the whole future of the people of Israel, He opened the immediate future of the Median Achaemenid Empire – and explained how it would create its own collapse in the future.

Daniel 11:1 In the first year of Darius the Mede, I arose to be an encouragement and a protection for him. And now I will tell you the truth. Behold, three more kings are going to arise in Persia. Then a fourth will gain far more riches than all of them; as soon as he becomes strong through his riches.

Daniel offered encouragement to the King Cyaxeres (Darius) about the immediate future of his kingdom, perhaps at some time when Darius thought it was being usurped. The encouragement was this: there shall stand up yet three kings – (Gabriel already spoke of Cyrus) who was now co-reigning; and after him three others should arise. Though not as familiar to many in our day, the Achaemenid Persian Empire (550–330 BC) was the largest kingdom the ancient world had seen to that time, extending from Anatolia and Egypt across western Asia to northern India and Central Asia. The rulers referred to are: 559-530 – Cyrus II the Great, 529-522 – Cambyses (son) who reigned seven years and five months; 521-486 – Darius I, the Great and 485-465 – Xerxes I (son). He was the fourth king that was prophesied to be "far richer" and that was demonstrated in his extended party in Esther 1 (where he was called Ahashverosh). The prophecy that he would "stir up against Grecia" was realized in battle after battle – and loss after loss by the Persians. Money couldn't buy him victory.

The historian Herodotus recorded that his army amounted to five million, two hundred and eighty-three thousand, two hundred and twenty men. Three years were invested preparing for the expedition against the Greeks, and Daniel foretold it all…Eight more rulers would follow in the Median Empire, but they would never best Greece, and were eventually overtaken by it… but that is no surprise, because Daniel foretold that as well!

What does this prophecy teach us? There are times a kingdom is not undone by others, but is destroyed by the ambitions of its own rulers. The richest and largest still hungered for more, and their insatiable desire for "just a little more" destroyed them. Greed is a killer force.

Part Three: "Buck Goat" rising: the coming rise of the Helenic Kingdom was predicted. (Alexander and the Diadoche – 11:2-4)

The details of the Median Kingdom are matched by the prophecy of the rise and fall of Alexander the Great as the Hellenic Kingdom swallows up the eastern Mediterranean and the Persian Gulf.

11:2 ...he will arouse the whole empire against the realm of Greece. 3 And a mighty king will arise, and he will rule with great authority and do as he pleases. 4 But as soon as he has arisen, his kingdom will be broken up and parceled out toward the four points of the compass, though not to his own descendants, nor according to his authority which he wielded, for his sovereignty will be uprooted and given to others besides them.

Swift in conquest, the Greeks swept the world, but their kingdom was quickly divided after the death of Alexander the Great. Don't miss the lesson here...

The lesson: **Even powerful and successful men can be cut down in short order**. A lifetime of accomplishment can be washed away as swiftly as a sand castle at the incoming tide. We cannot put trust in accomplishments, awards, fame and power – they are all temporal and fleeting.

Part Four: Divisions and Strife: the battles of Hellenic Monarchies (Seleucids and Ptolemies) are revealed (11:5-20).

A large section of Daniel 11, from 11:5-20 details a long litany of battles and conflicts between two Greek ruling households – one located in Egypt, the other is Syria. One is the noted "king of the south," the other "king of the north."

The historical detail can seem overwhelming in the text, but there are a number of insights that are worth considering when looking through this chapter.

The prophecy of Daniel 11 is both LONG and SIMPLE. It reveals the most detailed prophecy in the book and one of the longest in all of the Hebrew Scriptures, yet it is without symbolism.

Daniel 11 is EARTH BOUND. The text presents physical war, peace and treaties – not heavenly conflict.

Daniel 11 is CONFIRMED in history as written before the events:
- The historian Josephus Flavius (a younger contemporary to the Apostle Paul and other Apostles, died c. 100 CE) recorded that Alexander the Great read a copy of Daniel at the time of his annexation of Jerusalem in 332 BCE (Antiquities of the Jews XI, chapter viii, paragraphs 3-5).

- Furthermore, two ancient historical sources record that Ptolemy Philadelphos (308-246 BCE) commissioned the Greek translation of the Hebrew Bible (called the Septuagint or LXX) in the 3rd century BCE, and Daniel was included in the LXX collection.

- Finally, Daniel is also included among the Dead Sea Scrolls (1Q and 4Q) which date from about C 2nd BCE (the oldest manuscript is 4Q114, dating from the late 2nd Century BCE).

The simple lesson: God will offer just enough evidence to commend believers as He allows us to "uncover" the truth. Don't ask for PROOF, but don't think there is NO EVIDENCE either.

Part Five: the Template: a Seleucid ruler shows the pattern of hatred toward God's people (Antiochus IV – 11:21-35).

Daniel 11:21 In his place a despicable person will arise, on whom the honor of kingship has not been conferred, but he will come in a time of tranquility and seize the kingdom by intrigue. 22 The overflowing forces will be flooded away before him and shattered, and also the prince of the covenant. 23 After an alliance is made with him he will practice deception, and he will go up and gain power with a small [force of] people. ... 35 Some of those who have insight will fall, in order to refine, purge and make them pure until the end time; because [it is] still [to come] at the appointed time.

Daniel 11:21-35 sets up a TYPE that is later mimicked by an end time villain. Mentioned because of their rabid hatred of the Jewish people, two kings rise up in Israel's future that will apply pressure on the Jews. The first, Antiochus IV Epiphanes demonstrates an important lesson to God's people (11:21-35). A second "willful king" (Antichrist, 11:36-45) is exposed for his special cruelty and troubles for the Jewish people.

The lesson: **The enemy hates God, and hates anyone God makes promises to**. He wants to show that God cannot do what He claimed, and doesn't deserve the position He holds. He does this in grand scale – but he also does the same in my life. Satan tries to make me think that God doesn't lead well – and pushes me to show my independence from God. In my arrogance, I can even come to believe I know better than God about y future, my plans and my best path.

Part Six: the Destroyer: a future ruler – the hateful antichrist was described (Daniel 11:36-45)

1,600 years ago, the Bible scholar Jerome, who translated the Vulgate, wrote: Those of our persuasion believe all these things are spoken prophetically of the Antichrist who is to arise in the end time." (Jerome, *Romans*, p. 129)

This passage offers our first deep glance at four specifics regarding the Antichrist and his system. We know:

His **time** (36): He will be active during "the time of wrath." As Jesus made clear in Matthew 24, So when you see standing in the holy place 'the abomination that causes desolation, [that can't refer to Antiochus because that happened 200 years before Jesus spoke these words] spoken of through the prophet Daniel–let the reader understand–For then there will be great distress, unequaled from the beginning of the world until now–and never to be equaled again." Jesus says the Antichrist will be active during this time of great distress.

His **temperament** (37-39): He will be a charismatic, ambitious, egotistical, arrogant politician– that really narrows it down, doesn't it? Verse 37 says, He will show no regard for the gods of his fathers. That means he will reject his spiritual heritage and worship another kind of god: power, money, and military might. He may begin as a man of peace, but he becomes a vicious and cruel warrior.

The Apostle Paul wrote about the Antichrist in 2 Thessalonians 2:4: He will exalt himself over everything that is called God or is worshiped, so that he sets himself up in God's temple, proclaiming himself to be God. We should recognize the essence of sin is not atheism; it is self-worship. Basically, the man is a man of violence, a man of war and will be responsible for a renewal of war between parties in the Middle East.

His **territory** (40-44)

Daniel 11:40 suggests he will war in the Near East...in 41 He will also enter the Beautiful Land, and many [countries] will fall; but these will be rescued out of his hand: Edom, Moab and the foremost of the sons of Ammon. Skip down to verse 45. He will pitch his royal tents between the seas [the Mediterranean and the Dead Seas] at the beautiful holy mountain [Jerusalem]... He will ultimately set up his throne affirm some kind of peace treaty between Israel and her neighbors. In order to maintain this "peace" he will set up a residence in Jerusalem.

His **termination** (45)

Daniel 11:45 ...yet he will come to his end, and no one will help him.

During the seven years of the Tribulation, the Antichrist will be the lead dog in the pack. Listen to how John describes this devastating defeat of this demonic demagogue in *Revelation 19:20: But the beast was captured, and with him the false prophet who had performed the miraculous signs on his behalf. With these signs, he had deluded those who had received the mark of the beast and worshiped his image. The two of them were thrown alive into the fiery lake of burning sulfur."*

Here is the truth: **God is going to allow some wicked men and women to take advantage of His people – both Jews in the future and believers today**. Evil isn't winning, it is fulfilling its assigned role – and it will end when and how God says it will.

Part Seven: Free at Last: the restoration of the Jewish people was made clear (Daniel 12).

We'll be back here. It is worth noting the story doesn't end in the rise and fall of evil – but in the promise of God to fulfill His promises to His people... that is the essence of the reason for the glimpse ahead in the first place.

Israel's future is about His promises. Our lives are about His promises.

Do not despair when evil gains – God is in control of the story. His patience is a benefit to my lost friend – not an inability of His strong arm. **Do not complain when darkness rises** – God will used the dark threads in His needlework just as He uses the bright colors – to show Himself on the tapestry of human history.

Look into the dark cave with confidence.

- **The story is His.**
- **The glory is His.**
- **The victory is His.**

The promise is ours… and we celebrate it!

Shine the Light
Lessons in Daniel

Lesson Twelve: Daniel 10:1- 21 "Sock Puppets"

I have always been fascinated by puppets. I love marionettes in particular, as they were a staple of entertainment for nearly two thousand years in villages and towns of the western world. If you ever get the opportunity to travel to Palermo in Sicily, one of the oldest marionette puppet museums can be found in the "Opera dei Pupi" that opened in the thirteenth century, and still maintains some of the traditional shows and themes. The detail of each marionette, particularly that of the soldiers and courtiers is stunning.

I don't believe that I could operate something that complicated, but I do understand the principle of pulling strings, and manipulating the movements of the puppet. **My level of puppet operation lends itself better to "sock puppets" however.** If that were the level of skill required, I believe I could attain real accolades as a champion… but my dreams are probably misplaced. At any rate, **isn't it incredible how quickly we can transfer living character to something as simple as a sock or piece of paper-mâché?** We can watch a puppet "move", and listen to it "talk" as though it had its own personality. We KNOW that within it there is a puppet master's hand – but we seem to easily forget that when we are watching. Anyone who grew up on a diet of "The Muppets" will quickly agree…We seem mesmerized and quickly tricked into believing that controlled devices are "self-driven" beings – and that is a lesson we should not shake off too easily… In fact, our enemy counts on that trick in daily life to discourage us. Let me explain.

There is a verse in 2 Corinthians that I have come to believe was ABSOLUTELY TRUE when the Apostle Paul wrote it, but I am almost certain is NOT TRUE if he were walking through life with believers that inhabit the planet now. I don't believe Paul would write this if he knew the church and her people today... He was writing on the subject of forgiveness to one who was disciplined by the church and he made this passing comment in *2:11 ...so that no advantage would be taken of us by Satan, for we are not ignorant of his schemes.* Really? Paul said that people who served Jesus and traveled with him were able to see how the enemy was at work in the world – they could peer through the breach between the physical world and the spiritual world and spot the "puppeteer that was pulling many strings" behind events in their world... I find that amazing. In fact, if you look even deeper, you will find the ability to recognize the agenda of the hidden world was a key factor in his ability to stay encouraged when things weren't going well in his life and ministry.

Key Principle: We gain courage and proper perspective when we recognize the physical world is not the only world, and in fact, not the REAL world. What we see, feel, and experience, is often caused by something we cannot see from a spiritual world well hidden.

Paul knew he was primarily a spiritual being. He recognized and taught that the eternal and spiritual world is the real (or lasting) world, while the temporal world is the shadow we are passing through in our "earth time". That knowledge gave him strength and endurance – and it will do the same for us as well. **On our way to Daniel 10**, let's think about that truth and its implications for a moment....

Say what you want about the Apostle Paul... but the guy knew how to "take a punch" and stay on his feet until the

final bell rang. In 2 Corinthians 11:24 he offered a "quick trip down memory lane" of battles fought during his thirty one years of ministry on earth from the time he received Christ in 36 CE up to the time of his third mission journey that ended in 54 CE (when he was writing the account in 2 Corinthians). What an eighteen years! He wrote about the events…:

11:24 Five times I received from the Jews thirty-nine [lashes]. 25 Three times, I was beaten with rods, once I was stoned; three times, I was shipwrecked, a night and a day I have spent in the deep. 26 [I have been] on frequent journeys, in dangers from rivers, dangers from robbers, dangers from [my] countrymen, dangers from the Gentiles, dangers in the city, dangers in the wilderness, dangers on the sea, dangers among false brethren; 27 [I have been] in labor and hardship, through many sleepless nights, in hunger and thirst, often without food, in cold and exposure.

Wow! That **sounds like a mission brochure bound to get new recruits to sign up**, don't you think?

Here is my question…How did a guy passing through these kinds of tough persecutions keep an un-jaded perspective, and press forward toward honoring Jesus with his life regardless of the circumstances? He had some secret many of us don't seem to have – and yet both Paul and Daniel long before him shared it. Listen again as Paul wrote to Corinth to explain his encouraged heart in spite of his physical circumstance:

2 Corinthians 3:15 But to this day whenever Moses is read, a veil lies over their heart; 16 but whenever a person turns to the Lord, the veil is taken away…18 But we all, with unveiled face, beholding as in a mirror the glory of the Lord, are being transformed into the same image from glory to glory, just as from the Lord, the Spirit. 4:1 Therefore … we do not lose heart… 7 But we have this treasure in earthen vessels, so that the surpassing greatness of the power will be of God and not from ourselves; 8 [we are] afflicted in every way, but not crushed; perplexed, but not despairing; 9 persecuted, but not forsaken; struck down, but not destroyed... 11 For we who live are constantly being delivered over to death for Jesus' sake, so that the life of Jesus also may be manifested in our mortal flesh.... 16 ...we do not lose heart, but though our outer man is decaying, yet our inner man is being renewed day by day. 17 For momentary, light affliction is producing for us an eternal weight of glory far beyond all comparison, 18 **while we look not at the things which are seen, but at the things which are not seen; for the things which are seen are temporal, but the things which are not seen are eternal.** *(Emphasis R. Smith)*

Did you catch the **secret to his encouragement**? He focused, along with his companions, on the world NOT SEEN, because he knew it was the REAL WORLD. It would last eons after the physical world was nothing but a distant memory...In fact... he wasn't the only believer that got COURAGE and REINFORCEMENT from the other side of the veil – from the eternal and "spiritual" world. Great men and women of God know this secret – they recognize the NEED TO LOOK BEYOND the physical world to find the TRUTH about events. Daniel did it as well... in fact he was a great example of this idea...and that story is captured at the end of Daniel's writings.

Daniel 10

Let's take a few minutes and finish our studies in the book of Daniel by going to the chapter that should be LAST if the account were collected chronologically. It is organized thematically, therefore chapter 10 is not at the end – but in TIME and ORDER of events it SHOULD BE THE LAST chapter of the book – so we are looking at it to end our series..

Mourning Prayer (10:1-4)

Yet another story opened with the practice of Daniel to seek God's direction and understanding of life as he prayed. This time he also fasted, and was deeply struggling with a message from God. It wasn't that the message didn't make sense – it was simply a hard message to stomach. He wrote:

Daniel 10:1 In the third year of Cyrus king of Persia a message was revealed to Daniel, who was named Belteshazzar; and the message was true and [one of] great conflict, but he understood the message and had an understanding of the vision. 2 In those days, I, Daniel, had been mourning for three entire weeks. 3 I did not eat any tasty food, nor did meat or wine enter my mouth, nor did I use any ointment at all until the entire three weeks were completed. 4 On the twenty-fourth day of the first month, while I was by the bank of the great river, that is, the Tigris...

There are three specifics Daniel offered about the time he spent seeking God:

First, he reminded us of the period of time: (10:1a)

The year was 536 BCE, some sixty-nine years after Daniel was taken captive into Babylon. He was in his eighties, and near the end of his life. The time block was a full three weeks of mourning, fasting and praying to gain understanding of God's message. Note that Daniel took his query to God on his knees, and remained there. He sought and sought God's clarification and response. Need we ask why he was so very strong in his witness for so long, and under such extraordinary experiences?

Second, Daniel made clear the pains of trouble: (10:1b-2)

Sometimes we feel uncertain because we don't KNOW what God wants us to do about something. In Dan's case, that wasn't it! Daniel understood a vision from God, but suffered because he was troubled about how God was going to work. Have you ever been deeply troubled by God's Word? There are wonderful parts of the Word that relate to Heaven, blessing and God's powerful saving and transforming work in me – and I cherish those passages! Yet, there are also other places, where God speaks very specifically about those who reject Him – even those among people I love deeply – and those parts are hard to read when I have my friend or loved one in mind. If saved is a reality, then so is lost. If acceptance of Jesus and His work at Calvary changed my destiny, then I must also understand the direction I was already headed when it was changed, and acknowledge that many in my life are still on that path!

Third, Daniel specified the practice of seeking: (10:3)

Daniel set aside the good food that God provided him, and even the daily bathing and normal hygiene of his life. He didn't go out among people, and he waited on God. *Proverbs 27:9* offers these words: *"Perfume and incense bring joy to the heart, and the pleasantness of a friend springs from their heartfelt advice."* Daniel set aside the delights of this world to focus on the message from the other world. He took his spiritual life, and the Words of God about reality to heart – and God used him powerfully.

Magnificent Person (10:5-13)

Not only did Dan's journal tell us about his prayer, it also related the story of a "magnificent person" that visited him from the eternal world to help him grasp what God revealed, and allow it to inform him without wounding him further. Daniel described the visitor, detailed his response to the appearing one, and then offered us an opportunity to glimpse into the spiritual world of which he was a part.

First, look at the description of the visitor: (10:5-6)

Daniel 10:5 I lifted my eyes and looked, and behold, there was a certain man dressed in linen, whose waist was girded with [a belt of] pure gold of Uphaz. 6 His body also [was] like beryl, his face had the appearance of lightning; his eyes were like flaming torches, his arms and feet like the gleam of polished bronze, and the sound of his words like the sound of a tumult.

Bible students immediately catch the similarity to the vision of the Risen Christ found in Revelation 1, as John the Apostle met Jesus on Patmos. Many descriptions are so similar, that some students conclude this is the same person, but I don't think so. I believe this is an angelic servant that served in Heaven's Tabernacle and bore a resemblance in dress because of that function. The visitor was:

Clothed in linen (As in Rev. 1:13, where the description is "one who looked as a man with a robe that reached His feet.") He was girded with a golden sash as a priest was supposed to be in Lev. 16:4; and as Jesus was in Rev. 1:13b.

Though he appeared as a man, his color was clearly different than Daniel – with descriptions of his body "like beryl gemstone" (Tarsheesh: yellow gemstone as chrysolite; the color of the wheels of God's moving platform from Ezekiel's vision of chapter 1:16; as well as the color of part of the garb of Lucifer before his fall from Heaven – Ezekiel 28:13. That color seems to be an indicator of Heaven and beings from that place. Note that some of the foundation stones of the heavenly city were beryl – cp. Revelation 21:20).

- The face of the visitor shone as lightning. The description is not clear: was the visitor bright? Were they white in color as in Revelation 1:14?

- The visitor's eyes blazed with fire, just as we see in the description of Jesus in Revelation 1:14. This may denote a holder of God's revelation of truth, but clearly had something to do with the knowledge and understanding of the individual.

- The visitor's arms and feet appeared to be made of polished brass, and matches the description of Revelation 1:15 as Jesus' appearance.

- The visitor brought God's voice, as is indicated by the multi-voiced sound of the words of Jesus in Revelation 1:15.

Clearly, Daniel knew this wasn't a distant relative from his homeland, but a heavenly messenger, a revered visitor that required his complete attention.

Second, Daniel noted his response as a servant of God (10:7-11).

Daniel 10:7 Now I, Daniel, alone saw the vision, while the men who were with me did not see the vision; nevertheless, a great dread fell on them, and they ran away to hide themselves. 8 So I was left alone and saw this great vision; yet no strength was left in me, for my natural color turned to a deathly pallor, and I retained no strength. 9 But I heard the sound of his words; and as soon as I heard the sound of his words, I fell into a deep sleep on my face, with my face to the ground. 10 Then behold, a hand touched me and set me trembling on my hands and knees. 11 He said to me, "O Daniel, man of high esteem, understand the words that I am about to tell you and stand upright, for I have now been sent to you." And when he had spoken this word to me, I stood up trembling.

- Daniel made clear that he alone saw the visitor, but others experienced a dread that caused them to flee – and he was left alone with his Heavenly friend (10:7).

- He had been fasting, but just as John before Jesus, he experienced such a drain on his energy that he was totally without strength (10:8).

Don't miss this detail – because it is terribly important. **Strength in THIS WORLD doesn't denote strength in the other world.** Standing before a visitor of Heaven, men are drained of their physical might – for that might has little effect on the eternal world. Those who are mighty here must not anticipate that might to be great there. The kind of strength one exhibits in Heaven comes from a different source, and is manifested differently.

- Daniel notes that he had a discolored face. The blood drained from his coloring, as he collapsed into a deep sleep.
- Slumping down as if he fainted or fell into a sleep – he was face down (10:9) until set up on "all fours" (10:10) by the touch of the visitor.
- He stood when instructed to do so, but found himself trembling, without the ability to stop (10:11).

Finally, Daniel included the revelation brought by the visitor. (10:12-13)

The visitor arrived with purpose, and in response to Daniel's prayer. Listen to the account of the beginning of the conversation:
Daniel 10:12 Then he said to me, "Do not be afraid, Daniel, for from the first day that you set your heart on understanding [this] and on humbling yourself before your God, your words were heard, and I have come in response to your words. 13 But the prince of the kingdom of Persia was withstanding me for twenty-one days; then behold, Michael, one of the chief princes,

came to help me, for I had been left there with the kings of Persia."

There are two important details found in those words:

- First, Daniel's prayer was IMMEDIATELY heard (10:12) in Heaven. Though a battle exists in heavenly places during this time, the lone voice of one man in a room crying out to God reaches Heaven. Don't ever forget that!

- Second, the delay in the response was not in any way related to Daniel's piety, some lack in his person or prayer – but explained SOLELY by spiritual warfare in Heavenly places. The Archangel "Michael" is the noted one who (with much help) cast out Satan to the earth in Revelation 12:1-9 as the war eventually will take a turn in the future.

When Daniel mentions these "princes," we are left to wonder **who they are** and **what role they seem to play in the events which take place on Earth**. We have only shadows from God's revealed word, but it appears as though they are not human rulers, but angelic powers. In the case of Michael, he serves as Israel's "prince," in the Word, and is a faithful servant of God. The princes of Persia (10:13) and Greece (10:20) appear to be fallen angels, whose dominion is restricted to a particular geographical and political nation. This follows the pattern of Isaiah 14 and Ezekiel 28, where the descriptions of Satan are begun as odes to political rulers, and then the satanic power behind their moves is revealed in metaphoric terms. Don't forget, when demons encountered Jesus in Mark's Gospel, they begged Him not to cast them from "their country" (Mark 5).

If you continue reading, it becomes clear that there was a purpose for the arrival of the visitor that was declared (10:14):
Daniel 10:14 Now I have come to give you an understanding of what will happen to your people in the

latter days, for the vision pertains to the days yet [future].

Daniel had deep respect for the spiritual world, and his strength was sapped from him. His paralysis and anguish was expressed, as it was clear that he needed angelic help to bear up in this circumstance (10:15-18).

Daniel 10:15 When he had spoken to me according to these words, I turned my face toward the ground and became speechless. 16 And behold, one who resembled a human being was touching my lips; then I opened my mouth and spoke and said to him who was standing before me, "O my lord, as a result of the vision anguish has come upon me, and I have retained no strength. 17 "For how can such a servant of my lord talk with such as my lord? As for me, there remains just now no strength in me, nor has any breath been left in me." 18 Then [this] one with human appearance touched me again and strengthened me.

The account continued, as the prophet gained strength and encouragement from the visitor, and Daniel requested the visitor deliver his message (10:19):

Daniel 10:19 He said, "O man of high esteem, do not be afraid. Peace be with you; take courage and be courageous!" Now as soon as he spoke to me, I received strength and said, "May my lord speak, for you have strengthened me."

The visitor offered an important and unusual glimpse into the spiritual world before he departed (10:20-21):

Daniel 10:20 Then he said, "Do you understand why I came to you? But I shall now return to fight against the prince of Persia; so I am going forth, and behold, the prince of Greece is about to come. 21 However, I will tell you what is inscribed in the writing of truth. Yet there is no one who stands firmly with me against these [forces] except Michael your prince."

Obviously, the account is truncated, and we don't have everything that passed between the two – prophet and visitor. What we do have is incredible. We have one of the most clear glimpses through the veil over the spiritual world that we will see in the Word, as it relates to the active battle in that world.

Go back to the **beginning** of the whole account. It started with Daniel becoming aware, by God's power and revelation, of a **GREAT CONFLICT**. Something was brewing in heavenly places, and **Daniel was made aware of it**. It put him on his knees, kept him from his bath, and left him weak and hungry. The demonic world was at work pressing Cyrus the ruler and the angel came to tell Daniel that **mortal men of God could be knowledgeable and helpful in the conflict**.

The passage does not reveal any specific VISION of future events, or words of direction for the Jewish people. This story wasn't about the **FUTURE**, but about the **PERSPECTIVE** and **RECOGNITION** that the other world that is engaged in the fight right now. It is about grasping that MORE IS GOING ON THAN MEETS THE EYE. It is about knowing that our physical world is not the REAL WORLD, but merely exhibits the symptoms of a deeper world – a spiritual world. We gain courage and proper perspective when we recognize the physical world is not the REAL world. What we see, feel and experience is often caused by something we cannot see from the REAL WORLD.

That is why we cannot simply fight politically and expect to win back territories with truth – the battle isn't always being fought where you think it is. Prayerful engagement is a threat to those we battle against, while prayer-less political action is ineffective.

Listen thoughtfully and reflectively to the words of Paul to the Ephesian church. Don't recite the words in your mind. LISTEN to their message:

Ephesians 6:10 Finally, be strong in the Lord and in the strength of His might. 11 Put on the full armor of God, so that you will be able to stand firm against the schemes of the devil. 12 For our struggle is not against flesh and blood, but against the rulers, against the powers, against the world forces of this darkness, against the spiritual [forces] of wickedness in the heavenly [places]. 13 Therefore, take up the full armor of God, so that you will be able to resist in the evil day, and having done everything, to stand firm. ... 18 With all prayer and petition pray at all times in the Spirit, and with this in view, be on the alert with all perseverance and petition for all the saints...

Do you want the church to stand firm in the faith against the tsunami of moral compromise of our day? Spiritually, we must "armor up"! We must see the battle in Heavenly places, and drop to our knees. We must pray for ourselves and other believers – that God's church will persevere and fight in spiritual ways! We must ask God to give the churches strength, the believers, endurance, and power to stand against the pressure to buckle to the world's mold.

We gain courage and proper perspective when we recognize the physical world is not the REAL world. What we see, feel and experience is often caused by something we cannot see from the REAL WORLD.

- **Sometimes, the warfare looks like opposition to someone hearing about Jesus and salvation.** Paul warned in *2 Corinthians 4:4: The God of this age has blinded the minds of unbelievers. You try to* *share the Gospel, but feel like you hit a wall – because you did.*

- **Sometimes, you just feel incredibly guilty and condemned by things long forgiven by God.** You can't see it, but like Joshua the High Priest of Zechariah 3, Satan is lobbing mud at you in the spiritual world – that is why they call him "Accuser".

- **You hear about a tragedy or experience intense pain and even after many years of following Jesus, you find yourself suddenly doubting God's goodness.** You start muttering: "I don't know why I'm the only one who has this constant financial challenge!" or "I don't know why I should have kids who didn't follow what I told them." The deceiver may well be at work discouraging you.

- **One day you get so angry at someone that you just want to walk away for good.** You don't think about what you can accomplish together for God – just your personal peace (as if distance will fix everything). You forget the *Bible* revealed, *Don't let the sun go down while you are angry, and don't give the devil a foothold (Ephesians 4:27).*

Men and women, **the other world is at war, and we are seeing symptoms.** It isn't "spooky" and we shouldn't be embarrassed to admit the truth. We must look with knowledge and understanding. We must pierce through prayerfully. Not everything adds up here, because it didn't all happen here. The war ends when God declares it will, but the whole story is not yet told.

Don't miss the truth by focusing only on this world – that isn't where the secret is.

Other volumes in the series through the Bible are available through amazon.com and can be found by searching for:

"Dr. Randall D. Smith"

Free teaching resources are also available at:

www.randalldsmith.com

www.ingramcontent.com/pod-product-compliance
Lightning Source LLC
Chambersburg PA
CBHW071457040426
42444CB00008B/1381